ELTON JOHN & TIM RICE'S

AIDA

THE MAKING OF A BROADWAY MUSICAL

ELTON JOHN & TIM RICE'S

AIDA

THE MAKING OF A BROADWAY MUSICAL

TEXT BY *MICHAEL LASSELL*

A WELCOME BOOK

EDITIONS

NEW YORK

This book is dedicated to my parents, Catherine and Michael Lassell, for their commitment to love, and to the cast of AIDA for the same reason.—ML

For information address:
Disney Editions
114 Fifth Avenue
New York, New York 10011

Produced by:
Welcome Enterprises, Inc.
588 Broadway
New York, New York 10012

Editorial Director: Wendy Lefkon
Senior Editor: Sara Baysinger
Associate Editor: Rich Thomas
Project Manager: Jacinta O'Halloran
Designer: Jon Glick
Design Assistant: Katie Shaw

Library of Congress Cataloging-in-Publication Data
Lassell, Michael, 1947–
Elton John & Tim Rice's Aida : the making of the Broadway musical / Michael Lassell.
p.——— cm.
ISBN 0-7868-6484-2 (hardcover)
1. John, Elton. Aida. 2. Musicals–History and criticism. I. Title: Aida. II. Rice, Tim, 1944–
ML410.J64 L37 2000
782.1'4-dc21
00-031771

Printed and Bound in England
First Edition
10 9 8 7 6 5 4 3 2 1

OPPOSITE TITLE PAGE: Adam Pascal as Radames and Heather Headley as Aida.

CONTENTS

INTRODUCTION

Aida meets a new millennium.
RIGHT: Ensemble member Jody
Ripplinger in the runway
sequence in Act I.

PRECEDING PAGES: Radames'
slave boat sailing from Nubia
back home to Egypt.

ELTON JOHN AND TIM RICE'S *AIDA* OPENED at the Palace Theatre on Broadway at 6:30 P.M. on Thursday, March 23, 2000. Produced by Hyperion Theatricals, a division of the Buena Vista Theatrical Group Ltd. (under the direction of producers Peter Schneider and Thomas Schumacher), this *Aida* for a new millennium had a suitably grand opening night. There were red carpets, television cameras, guest celebrities, and a roar of approval from the audience at the end of the show so loud it startled the actors, who hugged one another on stage.

As the playgoers filed out of the historic building, the actors, some of whom have been working on *Aida* in its various manifestations for years, began descending from the stage almost in disbelief. The joy they felt at having opened *Aida* in New York was palpable. So was the spirit of affection, respect, mutual admiration, and gratitude they felt for one another. Despite the sweat, the fatigue, the occasional tears that were the bumps in *Aida*'s long road to 7th Avenue and 47th Street, these people loved each other. In fact, on opening night, ensemble members Kenya Unique Massey and Raymond Rodriguez, a talented couple who met when they were cast for the show's first tryout in Atlanta, announced they were expecting a baby.

It was in the same spirit of affection that Elton John threw a party for the entire *Aida* company before the opening night of the Chicago run. He wanted to thank the director, choreographer, music director, the designers, all their associates and assistants, the stage managers and their staff, the electricians, carpenters, seamstresses, dressers, and wig wranglers—not to mention the musicians—before he knew whether or not *Aida* would be a success. And a swell party it was.

8

I started observing this show in the spring of 1998, several years after its development began. My first appearance in the rehearsal halls at 890 Broadway in Manhattan was during dance casting sessions for the first fully mounted production of the show, when it was still called *Elaborate Lives: The Legend of Aida*. I attended New York rehearsals and then went south to Atlanta to sit in on technical and dress rehearsals, previews, and even the warm, rainy opening night at the Alliance Theatre. I began the process all over again in the spring of 1999 with a largely changed leading cast, a recharged script, and a new production team for a thoroughly revised concept that was put before audiences in Chicago late in 1999.

I've seen set models, costume sketches, and fight rehearsals; sat in on production meetings and post-rehearsal confabs. I've seen the show forty or fifty or sixty times, and I've interviewed, formally and informally, almost everyone involved with the production. It's been a rare privilege—not just because *Aida* is a great show, which I think it is, but because as a stranger in the midst of a sometimes daunting creative process, I have been so warmly welcomed by everyone, from top-of-the-food-chain executives to stage-door security guards at the Alliance Theatre in Atlanta, the Cadillac Palace in Chicago, and, finally, the Palace Theatre in New York City, my home town.

I was deeply impressed by what I saw in the course of *Aida*'s tricky birth, despite having worked in academic and regional theaters in many creative capacities. I even appeared once in a Broadway musical myself (all right, it was a Columbia University Summer Theater revival of *Little Mary Sunshine* in 1972, way uptown on Broadway). As a journalist, I've interviewed scores of actors, singers, dancers, playwrights, and designers who have made theater on the Great White Way. But I've never seen anything in thirty-five years in or around theaters to compare with the day-to-day making of Elton John and Tim Rice's *Aida*.

The book that follows is an attempt to capture some small part of one writer's experience as a fly on the rehearsal-room wall. For everything that is included, of course, much is left out—otherwise this volume would be the size of an encyclopedia. Since the creative folk involved with the show and this book want to

Broadway's newest star: Heather Headley as the slave princess Aida.

11

provide a published record that intimates (if it cannot imitate) the multidimensional experience of the live theater, the book is driven by photographs (and, yes, I confess: I was listening to the cast album while I wrote it).

This book is arranged in four chapters. These took their inspiration both from the logical process of putting on a show, and also—like every element of the production—from the story itself: the love between the captive princess, Aida; her captor, the Egyptian captain Radames; and Amneris, the pharaoh's daughter—perhaps history's first love triangle. Each of the four chapters focuses on triadic relationships.

Unfortunately for those of us who like life in neat categories, the processes described overlap constantly, overrunning the lines between and among time, place, and departments. Even during rehearsals it was not unusual for the ensemble to be rehearsing a dance number with the choreographer in one room while one of the lead characters worked out a major song with the music director in another, and yet other actors worked on a book scene with the writers and director in a third.

Chapter one, "The Story," looks at the time in which the tale is set, the way it exists in the present, and the way it functions in theatrical time. We've titled chapter two "Composition," by which is meant far more than the music. Think of it as the means of telling the story as it develops between the composer (Elton John), the lyricist (Tim Rice), and the playwright (or, in this case, playwrights, Linda Woolverton, David Henry Hwang, and Robert Falls).

Chapter two addresses the ways in which the talents who create the score and script work together, the primary focus here being the work that is done, at least in theory, before rehearsals begin.

Chapter three, titled "Production," concerns itself with the physical production of the play, the job of the designers working in their own mediums to realize the director's essential vision. The triangular relationship in chapter three consists (primarily) of director Robert Falls, set and costume designer Bob Crowley, and lighting designer Natasha Katz. (For the sake of clarity: Robert is always Robert Falls, and Bob is always Bob Crowley,

PRECEDING PAGES: Pharaoh (Daniel Oreskes) presides at the wedding of his daughter, Amneris, to his intended successor, Radames.

although they were generally referred to by the company in the course of production as "the Bobs.")

Chapter four, "Performance," tells the story of how the "text" (script, music, lyrics) becomes a live performance. This is the most complex chapter. Here the points of the triangle are the director, working with the choreographer (Wayne Cilento), the music director (Paul Bogaev), and, of course, the cast.

Finally, as the putative author of this book (almost as much a collaboration as *Aida* itself), I have to acknowledge the enormous assistance of some co-conspirators. First, my thanks to Disney and to the gentlemen at Hyperion Theatricals who were responsible for my having this opportunity: producers Peter Schneider and Thomas Schumacher, as well as Stuart Oken and Marshall B. Purdy. Thanks also to Ken Silverman and Michael Sanfilippo, for their many gestures of inclusion; to Lisa Edwards, for her cheerful attentions and kindnesses; to production supervisor Clifford Schwartz, for quintessential, but tender professionalism; and to associate director Keith Batten for insight, support, humor, and letting me check my E-mail on his laptop during rehearsals.

Thanks must also go to Wendy Lefkon of Disney Editions, an erudite, elegant, and enthusiastic editor, and to her colleagues, the indefatigable Rich Thomas and the always upbeat Sara Baysinger. The book's designer, Jon Glick, not only did a terrific job with the layouts, but he was uncommonly patient and flexible during the process. I am grateful, too, to the creative team of *Elaborate Lives*—Robert Jess Roth, Matt West, Stanley A. Meyer, and Ann Hould-Ward—for their time and fellowship.

Most of all, I want to thank Elton John, Tim Rice, Linda Woolverton, David Henry Hwang, Robert Falls, Wayne Cilento, Bob Crowley, Paul Bogaev, Natasha Katz, and the cast and company of *Aida*, for their gifts, their energy, their hospitality, their multifarious joys, and for being the most extraordinary teachers, which is one of the nicest things I can think of to say about anyone.

Michael Lassell
New York City
May 2000

"EVERY STORY, NEW OR ANCIENT,

BAGATELLE OR WORK OF ART,

ALL ARE TALES OF HUMAN FAILING,

ALL ARE TALES OF LOVE AT HEART..."

From "Every Story Is a Love Story" by Elton John and Tim Rice

CHAPTER ONE
THE STORY

THE STORY OF *AIDA*, THE CAPTIVE PRINCESS who is enslaved by an Egyptian captain and placed in the service of the pharaoh's daughter, enters European consciousness in 1871 via the opera *Aida* by Giuseppe Verdi. Then one of the most popular composers in Europe, Verdi at first resisted the invitation to create a showpiece for the opening of the Suez Canal. Yet, ever since the opus was completed, it has been a standard of the operatic repertory and a favorite with sopranos and tenors alike (in the early twentieth century, Enrico Caruso portrayed the love-torn Egyptian captain, Radames, at opera houses all over the world). The first musical version of *Aida* was an instant hit.

The story of star-crossed lovers along the banks of the Nile begins long before 1869. But it was in that year that the khedive of Egypt (the viceroy of the Turkish sultan who controlled Egypt at the time) instructed his inspector general of monuments to commission an opera for the 1870 opening of the canal that would change shipping (and politics) forever. The gentleman, one Auguste Mariette, created an outline for a libretto and turned to Camille du Locle, a fellow Frenchman, for help, reportedly suggesting Wagner, Gounod, or Verdi as composer. Du Locle pursued a reluctant Verdi, then fifty-seven years old, with his potent story (and a huge commission fee) until the maestro accepted, turning to the Italian librettist Antonio Ghislanzoni for his words, but only after his music was complete.

The opera debuted a year after the famous waterway, thanks to Verdi's hesitation and his perfectionism, but it was greeted as a work of art and passion as prodigious in its way as the canal was in the realm of engineering and science. Both the Suez Canal and Verdi's *Aida* have been with us ever since.

Verdi's librettist credited the story he had received from Mariette to a traditional tale "from the time of the pharaohs," a none-too-specific span of some thirty centuries or more.

So it is not possible to guess which pharaoh may have been on the throne at the time of the "real" Aida, if she ever existed, or which princess might have been the historical antecedent of Amneris. In fact, Mariette himself may very well have made up the story to please the khedive and to provide a European composer with some logical and lyrical point of departure for a

Two princesses worlds apart: Heather Headley as the Nubian slave Aida (OPPOSITE) and Sherie René Scott as Amneris, her mistress—and the pharaoh's daughter (BELOW).

*Aida re-imagines the ancient
tale of star-crossed young
lovers and tells it in a medium
that is part Broadway musical
and part rock concert.*

work based on a culture that was only partly understood at best and far from respected by its succession of overlords (Napoleon's soldiers, for example, used the Sphinx for target practice, which is why it no longer has a nose). The story of Aida, however, is a not implausible tale rooted in Egypt's history of enslaving virtually all the neighboring peoples of the Middle East.

Elton John and Tim Rice's *Aida*, with its book by Linda Woolverton, Robert Falls, and David Henry Hwang, retells for a modern audience a story that exists in the collective imagination by virtue of Verdi's opera. In the new version, the principal players remain the same: a princess, her enslaved handmaiden (who is also secretly a princess), and the man who loves and is loved by both.

"It's a mythic story of doomed love set against extraordinary times," says the production's director, Robert Falls. "But," he points out," it is a story for our own times set against battlefields, warring countries, and racial prejudice. It's as contemporary as today's headlines." The theme of star-crossed lovers is familiar through a tradition that includes Shakespeare's *Romeo and Juliet*, the source of *West Side Story* (just as Shakespeare's play was based on an earlier Italian Renaissance romance).

THE STORY OF *AIDA*

Aida, daughter of Nubia's King Amonasro, is captured by the Egyptian Captain Radames and his triumphant men. They find her along with a group of Nubian women near the second cataract of the Nile, perhaps near present-day Aswan.

The clearly spirited Aida is taken to Egypt, presumably to Memphis, the capital of Egypt since some time in the third millennium B.C., and given by Radames to Amneris, the daughter of the pharaoh. It has been decided by their fathers, the pharaoh and his chief minister, Zoser, that the two young people, having largely been raised together, will wed.

Unknown to any but his cadre of villains, however, is Zoser's plan to assassinate the pharaoh. Motivated by an insatiable appetite for wealth and a thirst for power, this corrupt politician has been slowly poisoning the monarch. Zoser intends to install Radames on the throne and to plunder the world in his son's name.

Although Radames and Amneris do love each other, they could not be more unalike. He is adventurous and wants only to explore the far reaches of the Nile. She is something of a "princess" in a modern sense: spoiled, self-centered, and to all appearances completely incapable of ruling Egypt. Both Egyptians come under the sway of the Nubian Aida, who despite her enslavement is every inch a noblewoman and a bit of an adventurer herself at heart.

22

The captured Aida (Heather Headley, OPPOSITE) is taken to Egypt by Radames on his Nile barge (ABOVE). Back home (BELOW), Radames (Adam Pascal) is met by his father, Zoser (John Hickok).

Radames begins to fall in love with Aida (and she with him). Meanwhile, Aida is enlisted by Radames' trickster servant, a Nubian adolescent named Mereb, to lead their captive countrypeople out of Egypt. Concurrently, the two princesses feel a growing kinship and form a bond of friendship and understanding that begins to strengthen them both.

Matters are complicated by the three fathers of the young lovers, who represent obligations to society that are more important than individual love: Radames and Amneris owe allegiance to Egypt; Aida, to Nubia. The emotional complexity and power of *Aida* come from this age-old dilemma: pure love at odds with duties to a higher purpose. The three central characters are not free to explore the meaning of their deep feelings: their public obligations conflict with the stirrings of their own hearts.

Amneris loves Radames in large part because he loves Egypt. Radames loves Egypt, but he has the soul of an explorer, not a monarch. Aida, guilt-ridden over having led a band of her women into slavery because of her own wanderlust, finds herself increasingly in love with the rapidly changing Radames, for whom she represents freedom—even though he is, in fact, her captor. (Aida's guilt increases when one of the Nubian women, Nehebka, goes willingly to die in her stead).

When Amonasro, Aida's father, is also captured and enslaved, she must renounce her love for Radames to take action for the sake of her people. Although Aida feels daunted by the prospect of leadership—Radames also shares this fear—she realizes that her devotion to her people is the greater love. Aida, Mereb, and the Nubian king plan his escape to take place during the wedding of Amneris and Radames, which has been announced publicly despite Radames' reluctance.

Aida is forced to action when her father, Amonasro (Tyrees Allen) is captured. LEFT: He tells her to forsake her Egyptian captain. OPPOSITE: Aida accepts the leadership of her people.

24

Aida goes to see Radames one last time. He tells her that he wants to renounce his impending marriage and run away with her. Although Aida would like nothing more, Amonasro's escape depends on Radames' marrying Amneris. Radames tells Aida that he will provide a boat to get her out of Egypt, thus unwittingly providing the means of escape for the king of Nubia, his country's enemy.

Unknown to Aida and Radames, Amneris overhears their pledge of love, her heart doubly broken, both by the man she loves and by her only true friend.

Zoser discovers the escape plot. Amonasro gets away, but Aida is caught and imprisoned along with Radames, who is now accused as a traitor. They are condemned to death and will be buried alive. Amneris' suffering has made her wise, however, as well as strong. With enormous respect for their love, Amneris orders Aida and Radames to be entombed together. She ascends the throne alone, forsaking the warlike reign of her father, while Radames and Aida ascend to the ranks of legends, their love becoming immortal.

Amneris (OPPOSITE) overhears her friends confess their undying love the night before her wedding. For crimes against Egypt, Radames and Aida (BELOW) must die.

27

THE BIRTH OF *AIDA*

Broadway productions have stories too, and the story of Elton John and Tim Rice's *Aida* dates back to 1994. *The Lion King* film was playing in movie theaters (the stage version had not yet been conceived). Disney was eager to work again with Elton John and Tim Rice, and the composer–lyricist team were likewise interested in pursuing their relationship with Disney. They had

enjoyed collaborating on the songs they wrote for the film (these and others they had written were later used in the score of Broadway's *The Lion King*). The Elton John and Tim Rice songs for *The Lion King* eventually garnered Oscar® and Grammy® awards for the two Brits.

"We were talking about what we could do with Elton and Tim," remembers Thomas Schumacher, president of Buena Vista Theatrical Group, who shares that title with Peter Schneider. (Buena Vista Theatrical Group is an umbrella that includes both Hyperion Theatricals and Disney Theatricals, which produced Disney's *Beauty and the Beast* and *The Lion King* on stage.) "Given the huge success of *The Lion King* film and the great relationship we had with Elton and Tim, you can imagine that we were excited about working with them again," agrees Peter Schneider.

Meanwhile, Schumacher and Schneider had acquired for their company the rights to a children's book by opera diva Leontyne Price. It retold the story of Princess Aida (a role Ms. Price had sung to great praise all over the world). Schneider and Schumacher had been considering it as an animated film and brought the idea up with John and Rice.

OPPOSITE: Composer Elton John with musical director Paul Bogaev.

TOP: Producer Thomas Schumacher with Elton John and director Robert Falls; RIGHT: Schumacher and Bogaev watch the ensemble at work.

29

"We weren't absolutely keen on doing an animated film right then," recalls Tim Rice, "we wanted a different challenge."

"Since Elton and Tim were eager to do something other than another animated film," Schneider remembers, "we thought, 'What about marrying them with *Aida* and doing it as a live musical?'"

"I remember having said, 'Give us something really dangerous,'" says Elton John, "and that's when Tom and Peter presented us with the idea of doing a brand new stage *Aida*."

"After all," says Schumacher, who frequently finishes Schneider's sentences, and vice versa, "since what was spectacular about the opera was the music, the most logical way to attack it artistically one hundred and thirty years later was to do something equally spectacular with the music."

"Well, that *was* dangerous," says Sir Elton, with a restrained grin, "because Verdi had already done it. We thought critics might throw bricks at us. But there were a lot of reasons for doing it. I had never written anything directly for the stage before, and I liked that. And the story is so good. It's a love triangle with political and spiritual overtones, timeless issues that are very important today. I just jumped at the chance."

Lyricist Tim Rice, whose stage credits include *Jesus Christ Superstar* and *Evita*, among many other Broadway and West End triumphs, was also attracted to the story. "Most musicals that work," he asserts, "have a great story—it's the most important thing to get right."

"And *Aida* is a tragic, beautiful story about the ultimate sacrifice, about dying for love," John agrees.

One significant difference between Verdi's *Aida* and his own, Elton John points out, is that "this one is not an opera. It's truly a pop musical, with spoken dialogue. There are black songs, very urban-based, rhythm 'n' blues, gospel-inspired songs, and kind of 'Crocodile Rock' songs, and ballads, of course.

"This is my version of what *Aida* should be in a modern way," says the songwriter. "After all, Verdi's music was modern, too, when it was written."

Starting from scratch with the ancient story, doing it as a piece primarily for adults and not specifically for children, presented the opportunity of introducing an important and timely story to people who might never attend an opera. And so work began.

An Aida *for the Rock Age: Sherie René Scott in the runway sequence of Amneris' "My Strongest Suit" number in Act I.*

"I KNOW EXPECTATIONS ARE WILD AND ALMOST

BEYOND MY FULFILLMENT, BUT THEY WON'T HEAR

A WORD OF A DOUBT OR SEE SIGNS OF WEAKNESS.

MY NIGH-ON IMPOSSIBLE DUTY IS CLEAR . . . ."

From "Dance of the Robe" by Elton John and Tim Rice

CHAPTER TWO

COMPOSITION

LIKE MOST BROADWAY PRODUCTIONS, *AIDA* went through a process of development before it settled into the show that opened on Broadway. There were three workshops, a first production in Atlanta and another that opened in Chicago and which, with major changes, went on to New York. In some senses, the development of *Aida* was much like the open-out-of-town model that was once standard, although the producers were cautious in scheduling each step of the *Aida* process.

What makes Thomas Schumacher and Peter Schneider ideal to head the Disney theater division is their shared background in not-for-profit theater and their work on the latest successful wave of Disney's musical animated films. But *Aida* is their first full-scale original Broadway musical created specifically for the stage. Disney's other live shows—*Beauty and the Beast*, *The Lion King*, and *The Hunchback of Notre Dame* (now playing in Berlin)—are all based on films that were created in private and never seen by the public until they met the producers' expectations. A Broadway show that opens "on the road" is a much more public affair.

When the decision was made to go forward with *Aida* for a stage production rather than an animated film (this one produced under the new banner of Hyperion Theatricals, to distinguish it from the G-rated family fare the name *Disney* implies), Leontyne Price's book was put aside. The producers hired Linda Woolverton, who wrote the stage version of *Beauty and the Beast*, to create an original script. Her mandate in collaborating with Robert Jess Roth, who directed *Beauty*, was not to start from Verdi, but from the original Egyptian story.

Aida is therefore as original as most of the work of Rodgers and Hammerstein (*Oklahoma!*, for example, is based on Lynn Riggs's play *Green Grow the Lilacs*), or, for that matter, most of the popular, enduring hits of Broadway history. For *Porgy and Bess*, the Gershwins turned to DuBose Heyward to adapt his *Porgy*, a play based on his own novel. *Hello, Dolly!* draws on Thornton Wilder's *The Matchmaker*, a revision of an earlier Wilder play, which was an Americanization of an 1842 Viennese version of an 1835 British antecedent. Steven Sondheim's *A Little Night Music* was inspired by Ingmar Bergman's *Smiles of a Summer Night*; and, as previously noted, *West Side Story* is a retelling of Shakespeare's *Romeo and Juliet*.

Heather Headley as Aida: It is the slave princess, not her lover, who is the central character of this Aida.

35

"We had a lot of meetings at the beginning to get the plot right," remembers Tim Rice. "There were some things in the story that I'd taken for granted, because in an opera, the music carries the emotions of the characters, whereas in a musical with a book, the story line has to be complete."

One of Woolverton's innovations was to change Aida's homeland from Ethiopia (as in the opera) to Nubia. "I took a lot of inspiration from historical research," she explains, "and Nubia was very much a part of the history of Egypt. The Egyptians just absorbed Nubia and took credit for all the cultural richness they found there."

Most importantly, Woolverton and Roth firmly established Aida as the central character of this story, emphasizing her dilemma as a woman torn between passion for her lover, deep affection for her mistress, and an unshakable sense of duty to her people. Woolverton went back beyond the beginning of the opera's action—when Radames is already in love with Aida. The writer asked the question, "How would a slaveowner come to fall in love with a slave girl, and how could she fall in love with him?"—which is, in many regards, both a more interesting and more contemporary approach.

Another of Woolverton's innovations was to equalize the love triangle (and heat up the tragic dimension) by having Aida and Amneris become friends. "The relationship between the women was very important to me," the writer says. "To have Amneris be a shrew who is yelling at Aida for two hours just didn't seem right to me for this century. I wanted to re-create Amneris in such a way that we could gradually get to know her and what she's about."

Woolverton worked on the script, creating the scene dialogue up to the point where she thought a song should go. "Then I'd leave Tim a blank page," she remembers, "well, I scribbled down a lot of things that I thought the song should say. Soon Tim would send back these gorgeous song lyrics that were exactly the things I was thinking about but not expressing."

Verdi insisted on finishing the entire score of his *Aida* before turning it over to his librettist for lyrics. But Elton John doesn't work that way. "Elton always puts his tunes to the lyrics, instead of the other way around," says Tim Rice.

"Tim wrote the songs in order," Elton John reports, "which is how I worked on the *Captain Fantastic* album with Bernie Taupin. We had to shift some of the songs around later, but that helped me enormously."

The men in the ensemble perform "Another Pyramid" (BELOW), while Amneris (Sherie René Scott) and her handmaidens deck themselves out in "My Strongest Suit" (OPPOSITE).

Surprisingly, given the tragic scope of *Aida*, the first two songs Rice wrote were not deeply moving ballads, but two relatively comic numbers: "Another Pyramid," the evil Zoser's rock riff about his conspiracy to poison the pharaoh, and "My Strongest Suit," the Motown-inspired dance number that introduces Princess Amneris. (The songs were shifted in their order as changes were made to the script and the production, and they do not fall in first and second place in the score in the finished show.)

But other than lyrics that are written to explain or further the plot, just where do Rice's words come from? Does he have favorites? Are there words that won't work in a song at all?

"I don't have a particular strategy," the veteran of many Broadway musicals confesses. "I mean, I sit down with a cup of coffee and sharpen my pencil and all of that, but what happens next has just evolved over the years. I mean with a comic song, there's virtually no word that can't be used. With a romantic song, there are plenty.

"But then again, my working method changed a lot when I started working with Elton because I'd never written lyrics on their own before. It was the first time I had to sit down and think the lyrics up independent of their melodies. Most of my lyrics have been written to tunes that already exist, which is quite fun because for a brief spell, you are the only person in the world who's heard that song. You finish it, and you've got the tune, and you play the tape that this guy's given you, and you sing along with it, and you sing 'Don't Cry for Me, Argentina' or whatever, and you think, Nobody else in the world has heard this. That's quite fun.

"Working with Elton, I write a lyric, and more often than not, when I've finished it, I go to the piano and play a little tune of my own just to see if it sings. Because sometimes you can write what is technically or emotionally or linguistically quite a good lyric, but it may not be very singable. So I write a little country-and-western tune or something, and I sing along. And I get quite attached to this tune usually. And then, I fax the song to Elton. And three days later, I hear back an incredibly different tune from the one I was playing. And I usually think, Well, I preferred my own tune, just because I got so used to it. And so I play it again, and I think, No, Elton's tune is brilliant."

Pharaoh's Chief Minister, Zoser (John Hickok), is slowly poisoning the pharaoh to clear a place on the throne for Radames.

MUSICAL NUMBERS

ACT I

EVERY STORY IS A LOVE STORY
Amneris

FORTUNE FAVORS THE BRAVE
Radames and the Soldiers

THE PAST IS ANOTHER LAND
Aida

ANOTHER PYRAMID
Zoser and the Ministers

HOW I KNOW YOU
Mereb and Aida

MY STRONGEST SUIT
Amneris and Women of the Palace

ENCHANTMENT PASSING THROUGH
Radames and Aida

MY STRONGEST SUIT (reprise)
Amneris and Aida

DANCE OF THE ROBE
Aida, Nehebka, and the Nubians

NOT ME
Radames, Mereb, Aida, and Amneris

ELABORATE LIVES
Radames and Aida

THE GODS LOVE NUBIA
Aida, Nehebka, and the Nubians

ACT II

A STEP TOO FAR
Amneris, Radames, and Aida

EASY AS LIFE
Aida

LIKE FATHER LIKE SON
Zoser, Radames, and the Ministers

RADAMES' LETTER
Radames

HOW I KNOW YOU (reprise)
Mereb

WRITTEN IN THE STARS
Aida and Radames

I KNOW THE TRUTH
Amneris

ELABORATE LIVES (reprise)
Aida and Radames

EVERY STORY IS A LOVE STORY (reprise)
Amneris

39

Once Elton John had lyrics, he could begin to write the tunes. "The way Elton works," says music director Paul Bogaev, "is to take a lyric into the studio and to work out an idea of rhythm and then to compose the melody and lay down tracks at the same time."

"At one point," remembers the composer, "I had Tim in the studio in Atlanta, where I live. I was laying down tracks with my bass player and percussionist and Guy Babylon, who plays keyboards in my band. And Tim was right there in the back room writing into the computer. It was so exciting. There was a lot of momentum. I can't write a good song unless I have a good lyric. Tim's had great experience writing for the stage. I haven't. His experience helped me enormously."

Linda Woolverton remembers the first time she heard the music. "It was in Elton's studio in Atlanta," she recalls the week before opening night on Broadway. "And it was so adorable, because he was so nervous and shy about it. It was the first time he had played the music for anyone."

Although Rice had worked from prompts in Linda Woolverton's developing script, many of the lyricist's songs come from his own heart, and that's particularly true of "Elaborate Lives," the love song in which Radames and Aida finally confess their love to one another and surrender to their growing passion.

"'Elaborate Lives' is very much based on what I really feel," says Rice, "which is a rare chance in a show because for many of the songs I write for musicals, I'm writing only from the character's point of view. This is one of the few songs where I actually sat and wrote exactly what I feel: 'We all lead such elaborate lives.' For 'Easy as Life,' on the other hand, I tried to imagine how a woman would feel when everything has gone wrong, everything has collapsed, and she has to give up the one thing she loves most for 'another kind of love.'"

Once the first act and its songs were written, the creative team put together its first workshop, in April of 1996. "We worked for three or four weeks in New York," remembers Stuart Oken, creative executive for Disney's theater operations, "and we did it just for ourselves, just using music stands, like a staged reading."

Aida (Heather Headley) and Radames (Adam Pascal) are drawn to each other and finally confess their mutual love in "Elaborate Lives" near the end of Act I.

40

Musical director Paul Bogaev has been involved with Aida *since before its first workshop.*

There were six songs completed for the first workshop, and Paul Bogaev had worked up orchestrations for two of them on piano and sequencer (which replicates the sounds of various orchestral instruments). One, a gospel-inspired "The Gods Love Nubia," remains pretty much the same on Broadway as it was at the first workshop. More songs would, of course, have to be written; some would move around as the book evolved—some more than once. Some of the songs would come to be sung by other characters than the ones for whom they were written.

"The first workshop was very comic," Linda Woolverton remembers," and, indeed, getting the tone of the show right was one of the greatest areas of concern all through the process. Would the lovers live happily ever after, or would they die in a tomb, as in the opera. It was decided to continue on the project, to see what the solutions to the problems were. A second workshop was held of both acts of the play in November of 1996.

"Once we could look at it and hear it," Thomas Schumacher says, "we could see what needed to be done. There were things we really liked and things we didn't." The creative team went back to the drawing board, made adjustments, and did the show again at a third New York workshop in the spring of 1997 that was more fully staged than the first two.

"That was a lot like the traditional backers' audition," says Schumacher, "when in the normal course of theater events, you're trying to get people to invest in a show. We weren't going to have any other investors, but we did need to see what needed to be added or eliminated to play to the strength of the material."

After the final workshop, it was decided to mount a production, teaming up with a nonprofit theater somewhere outside of New York. That theater turned out to be the Alliance Theatre in Atlanta. The production would, in fact, be a production of the Alliance Theatre Company, the artistic director of which is Kenny Leon, a vital theater force who is well thought of both in Atlanta and throughout the country. Disney provided "enhancement" money (the cost of the production envisioned exceeded the Alliance's usual production budget). A creative team was hired, a cast assembled, and work began for an opening scheduled for a limited run in Atlanta, from September 17 to November 8, 1998.

The show was titled *Elaborate Lives* after John's favorite song in the score. Among its lead actors would be Heather Headley, who had played Nala in Disney's *The Lion King* on Broadway, who was cast as Aida, and Sherie René Scott, a veteran of *Rent* and *The Who's Tommy*, as Amneris. (Both of them would survive the next eighteen months of development to open on Broadway; Scott has been involved since the first workshop).

Schneider and Schumacher had always hoped to bring *Aida* to Broadway, but they took a wait-and-see approach. "The idea," says Peter Schneider, "was that if we partnered with a regional theater, we could do a production without all the financial and other pressures of going directly to Broadway. And there was a chance, if we just loved that production, we could move it to New York at a later date."

But no specific plans had been made for the show beyond the Atlanta run: the actors' contracts were only for Atlanta; no Broadway theater had been booked. And although the show was virtually sold out to cheering Atlanta crowds, the producers stepped back for sober reflection.

ABOVE: Aida meets Amneris;
BELOW: The three lovers in
"Not Me" in Act I.

"Atlanta was a great experience for us," says Thomas Schumacher, "because it gave us the chance to get the show up to see if it would fly. And what was really clear in Atlanta was that the fundamental material of the show was there. It worked. Now, it's legendary that we had technical problems in Atlanta," he continues, "but that turned out to be a hidden benefit—because we were able to see the production stripped down to its barest, simplest form."

In fact, at the first preview of *Elaborate Lives*, the large, central set piece—a pyramid that operated via computer, lasers, and hydraulics—hit a glitch early into the first act and the action of the show came to a complete stop. This became known among the cast as "The Night the Lights Went Out in Georgia."

"I ran into the tech booth," recalls Schumacher, and said to Alan Hall, who was the production stage manager, 'We have to send these people home.' And Alan, who had stage-managed thirty-two Broadway musicals, said, 'I have never sent an audience home in my life, and I'm not going to start now. So please leave the booth because between 8 and 11 P.M., this is my show,' and he sent me out. He then set up a semicircle of chairs in front of the set and had the cast sing and act the entire show from the top in a concert version.

"Now the cast had never done the show this way. Everyone in the ensemble was dressed in whatever costume they had last appeared in or were about to appear in, and they just did the entire show, both the songs and the scenes. It was very, very powerful, and the audience went nuts."

The pyramid failed on opening night, too, in the presence of the local and national press, and it was clear by then that whatever the future of *Aida*, this expensive piece of stage equipment would be history. Despite its popularity, the Atlanta production got only mixed reviews. "The music got strong reviews," remembers Schumacher, "as did some of the cast members, Heather and Sherie in particular."

"The show in Atlanta was not completely right," recalls Tim Rice, "but there were things in it that were very good, indeed. But that's what tryouts are for. Sometimes the route to success is circuitous."

Two women: Aida (ABOVE) is independent, an adventurer; Amneris (OPPOSITE) seems spoiled and insubstantial.

44

"When we stepped back to get some distance from it," says Peter Schneider, "we had to ignore the fact that the music was powerful and the audience got quite whipped up by it. We had to decide if this was the show we were going to take to New York or if we wanted to do more work."

"Rob Roth loved this music and the show," says Schumacher. "He and his original creative group—which was the same group that created *Beauty and the Beast*, now in its seventh year on Broadway—developed the show and shaped the script and did all the fundamental work to get the show up on its feet. It was Rob's idea to approach the show as a cross between a traditional Broadway show and a rock concert."

"The music was excellent," agrees Schneider, "but *Elaborate Lives* didn't quite catch the emotional intensity of the story." As painful a decision as it was, we decided to go back to square one with a different creative team that could come at the material from a new place and with new energy to take the show to Chicago and then on to New York." "It was a difficult decision to ignore one standing ovation after another in Atlanta," says Schneider,"and to move forward with different people on the creative team."

At the suggestion of their creative affairs colleague Stuart Oken, Schneider and Schumacher hired Robert Falls as the show's new director. The artistic director of the Goodman Theatre in Chicago, Falls had directed a production of Arthur Miller's *Death of a Salesman*, which he subsequently moved to Broadway, and he was already talking with Schneider and Schumacher about an altogether different project. (Falls would later win a Tony for his directing job on *Salesman*.)

Choreography was assigned to Wayne Cilento, an original member of the cast of *A Chorus Line* (as Mike, he originated "I Can Do That"). Cilento had won a Tony, too, for his choreography of *The Who's Tommy* and was a nominee for *How to Succeed in Business Without Really Trying* with Matthew Broderick. On the design side, Tony-winning designer Bob Crowley—everyone's first choice—agreed to create both sets and costumes. Remaining

on board after Atlanta were lighting designer Natasha Katz, musical director Paul Bogaev, and sound designer Steve C. Kennedy.

As new and intentionally simpler sets and costumes were built, the show went back into rehearsal. Heather Headley and Sherie René Scott continued as Aida and Amneris (as did several key members of the ensemble). Adam Pascal of the original cast of *Rent* joined the cast as Radames, bravely entering waters where his two leading ladies already had some tidal confidence.

But the set wasn't the only thing that was to change: the script needed rethinking, too, and Robert Falls would be given latitude to rewrite as well as direct. The tone of the show, the interplay of comedy and tragedy, was still at issue.

"*Aida* is a musical piece about people who are enslaved," says Falls, and "you can't make too many jokes about that, although there are a few. Remember that *A Funny Thing Happened on the Way to the Forum* is also about slavery, but its story is told in comic terms." *Aida* was attempting to integrate the comic and tragic, the entertaining and the deeply emotional.

"When I first heard the Elton John demos," says Robert Falls, "I was knocked out by the material and the music. I was surprised and deeply moved by the score, by its passion and depth. I thought it was a rock-solid and beautiful story. I mean, I believe in love. People fall in love and commit themselves despite extraordinary pressures not to be together. *Aida* is a very mature, serious, erotic, and political love story—in the classic sense of *Tristan and Isolde* or *Romeo and Juliet*. It is intimate but epic, and I responded to that."

"*Aida* is a tragic love story," says Thomas Schumacher, "but also much more than that. It also has enormous wit and sophistication. That's why we offered Robert Falls the show. He was the right person to bring *Aida* from where it was to the production we knew, or hoped, could be made from the material."

Aida's ultimate director, Robert Falls (here rehearsing with Adam Pascal in New York) helped reshape the story after Atlanta.

Although Robert Falls was a well-known regional theater director, he had never before directed a Broadway musical (nor, for that matter, had Julie Taymor before Disney hired her to direct The Lion King at the New Amsterdam Theatre). Immediately prior to signing on to Aida, Falls had directed a stunning fiftieth anniversary production of *Death of a Salesman* in Chicago, which subsequently moved to Broadway and won him a Tony for best direction. Arthur Miller's play is often cited as the only authentic tragedy ever written by an American—although Falls has joked since his Aida assignment that he tried to insert some song and dance numbers into the play.

Apocryphal as that story clearly is, Robert Falls loves musical theater. "When I was very young," the director remembers, "I had a puppet theater, and I would do *My Fair Lady* and *The King and I*. It was the first theater I ever directed." More importantly, Falls had been intimately involved in developing new plays and reinterpreting classics. And he was determined to use his experience in the not-for-profit theater to avoid the many pitfalls on the often-steep road to Broadway success. Particularly, he did not want to lose the story in the clichés of the Broadway musical idiom.

"I did not approach *Aida* as a BIG BROADWAY MUSICAL," the director says, using his voice to indicate all caps, "even though it is one. I approached this material the way I approach everything, which is to work with the collaborators to create something authentic, something that's beautiful and spectacular but that, at

Director Robert Falls and associate choreographer Tracy Langran Corea in rehearsal with Heather Headley and Adam Pascal.

48

heart, is always true to the story, which in this case is theatrical, modern, and deeply serious."

And what he means by serious, he explains, is that "every moment is explored for its reality. I think you can create real sentiment and real humor by taking a work seriously. At the same time, I believe in entertainment."

To balance the antic and profound (the yin and yang of the dramatic art expressed in the joined comedic and tragic masks of Greek theater), Falls drew on Shakespeare. "I think that a Broadway musical can accommodate the same style shifts that Shakespeare can," he suggests. "You can have tragedy and comedy side by side." He admits, though, that finding the right tone and the right interplay between them was difficult.

49

Playwright David Henry Hwang in rehearsal (BELOW): Writing the book includes drawing a delicate line between comedy (Amneris in the spa, ABOVE) and drama (Zoser and Radames during "Like Father Like Son," OPPOSITE).

Falls began work on the post-Atlanta *Aida* by going to work on the script, doing his own draft to lay out his ideas. These included questions of character motivation, of relationships among the characters, and of tone. Specifically, recalls Thomas Schumacher, "Bob Falls wanted to avoid the forced and confusing 'happy endings' we tried in Atlanta or the ultimate lack of clarity in Atlanta's final version." Then the producers brought in playwright David Henry Hwang, Tony-winning author of *M. Butterfly*, to work as Falls's writing partner.

During the rehearsal period before the Chicago opening, certain questions were addressed and readdressed: Why should Aida fall in love with her captor? Why should he fall in love with a slave and give up the throne of Egypt for her? Why should Amneris, so seemingly frivolous on first glance, open up and show her truer nature to her servant? If Amneris has to be a strong leader at the end of the play, where does she find her strength? What is the effect of his love for Aida on Radames, and what effect does her love for him have on Aida?

"Clearly," says David Hwang, "Bob Falls's vision was to make it a more serious script. And he wanted to make the show more fluid, not just in the physical production, but also in terms of the relationships between the characters and of the relationship of the book to the other elements, the dance and the music."

50

Among the changes that moved the play toward serious adult fare was the reconception of Radames' wily Nubian slave. In Atlanta, the character was called Nekhen. He was conceived as a joke-telling twelve-year-old and was played by the prodigiously talented Scott Irby-Ranniar, who originated the role of Young Simba in Broadway's *The Lion King*. By the time rehearsals for Chicago began early in 1999, Nekhen had become Mereb, sufficiently older to be considered a man rather than a boy. Actor Damian Perkins was cast in the role.

But changes were legion. Much of Linda Woolverton's original structure remained, but many lines were rewritten time and time again, sometimes returning to the original when nothing better was found. The rewriting process in rehearsal, Hwang remembers, was "very, very fluid. Sometimes Bob made a change, sometimes I did. And it's been a real learning experience. When you write a play, the words are all you have. But here, there's incredible integration of music and dance, so the working method is very different. Sometimes we don't even need words because we have music and dance."

One decision the writers made early was to be willing to try anything. The original script of the show contained a letter of apology that Amneris was attempting to write to Radames, but she is having difficulty finding the words. Amneris convinces Aida to write the letter, and Aida reads it to Radames: the words and feelings are Aida's, although the letter comes nominally from Amneris. Just who was writing the letter and what the letter might be saying and who was singing it to whom and at what place in the play this might happen were all changed many times. In the final Broadway version, the letter is read by Aida in Act II; it is written by Radames, and he sings it to her ("Radames Letter.")

The production that opened in Chicago on December 9, 1999, was a far tighter, more grown-up play than the one that had opened in Atlanta the previous year, and once again audience reaction was strong. Once again, however, the creative team knew there was more work to do.

"Unlike the usual out-of-town tryout," says Robert Falls, "we did not work on the show after we opened in Chicago. We just let the cast run it without interference for eight weeks. And what we gained by that was a totally bonded cast with an enormous new confidence in their ability to perform the show, and the ability of the show to move an audience."

The sketch for Mereb's "How I Know You" costume (ABOVE) the actor (Damian Perkins, OPPOSITE) in what was eventually made for the character.

53

Built into the Chicago-to-Broadway schedule was a three-week hiatus for the cast and another three weeks of rehearsal in New York before moving into the Palace Theatre. But the creative team did not even wait until the show closed in Chicago to brainstorm. On the last weekend of the run, they met around the clock to decide what would have to change.

"The two major areas of concern," Thomas Schumacher summarizes, were the relationship between Aida and Radames and making it believable that she would fall in love with him."

A new song, it was decided, had to be written for Radames' entrance ("Fortune Favors the Brave") to establish his character. That meant new lyrics, a new melody, and new orchestrations. A fully staged ballet in which the Egyptian soldiers capture the Nubian women was cut in order to simplify the opening of the show. Everyone agreed that "Enchantment Passing Through," sung only by Radames, needed to be a duet for Radames and Aida.

For musical as well as dramatic reasons, Rice suggested that "Our Nation Holds Sway," a fully-staged ensemble scene at the end of the first act be cut and replaced by "The Gods Love Nubia" from the second. This meant that instead of seeing the arrival of the captured Nubian king (as in the opera), the audience now hears about it along with the slaves in the Nubian camp.

It was suggested, and seriously considered, to cut the entire runway sequence from Amneris' "Strongest Suit" number because it broke the narrative line. Others thought the scene was just too flat-out enjoyable to cut, and altogether appropriate given the composer of the show, himself a serious fan of high fashion. If, however, the runway was to survive, it would need new costumes for the ensemble women, an expenditure of thousands of dollars.

Every day, the cast worked at providing the audience what it needed to receive from the narrative and to keep the show entertaining without the show-business aspects overpowering or obscuring the love story. The challenge was to tell this tale in a way that made people want to weep as well as to get up and dance, to sing along but to sit back and reflect.

"What you wind up seeing," says Elton John, "are three characters in the process of maturing because of their love for one another. And being willing to give up everything for love changes you forever."

Amneris (Sherie René Scott) offers herself up to be dressed for her wedding, even after overhearing Radames with Aida, in "I Know the Truth" (Act II).

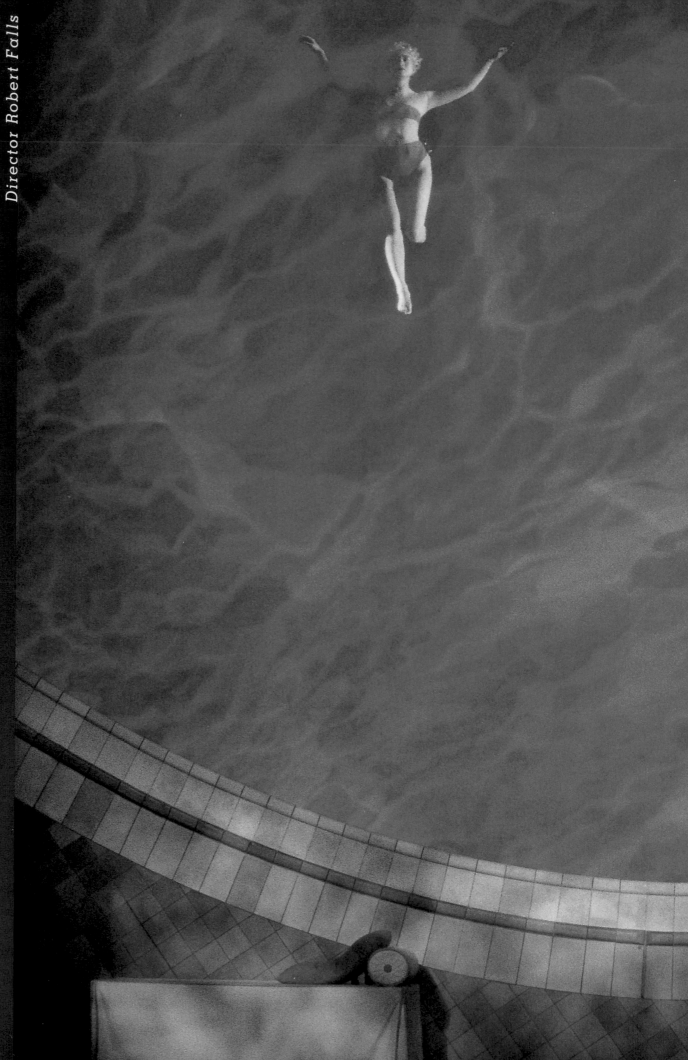

"CREATING A NEW MUSICAL IS A TRICKY THING

AND IT CAN'T JUST BE ONE PERSON'S VISION.

THE COLLABORATION IS VITAL."

Director Robert Falls

CHAPTER THREE
PRODUCTION

F OR ANY PLAY," SAYS *AIDA*'S DIRECTOR, Robert Falls, "the primary job of the director is to tell a story. In musicals, the tools you have to tell that story are the choreography and music, the actors and visuals—the sets, costumes, lights."

For the visuals of *Aida*, the producers turned to Irish-born Bob Crowley. Crowley was nominated for two Tony Awards in 1999, one for designing the Kevin Spacey *Iceman Cometh*, the other for *Amy's View*, starring Dame Judi Dench. He had already won a Tony for *Carousel* at Lincoln Center. His sense of adventure and his extraordinarily theatrical vision made him a perfect choice for a modern telling of the ancient story.

"Bob Crowley is a genius," says Robert Falls flatly, "one of the best designers working anywhere in the world. He's done a lot of opera and was head designer for the Royal Shakespeare Company for years. We approached the design of this *Aida* the same way we would approach Verdi's *Aida* or *Antony and Cleopatra*, which is to say, as a serious work for the stage.

"Visually," Falls continues, "we wanted to create our own Egypt, a contemporary one that draws on the runways of the fashion world as well as on the ancient silhouette of the Nile. And we wanted to mix in the Asian, Middle Eastern, and Indian influences that were coming into that region of the world."

"I try to find the emotional arc of the piece," explains Crowley, who is known for his nonrepresentational style of design. "I try to visualize a color or texture or image that supports the dramatic action. Bob Falls and I had a very similar, perhaps instinctive take on the piece, which had to do with stripping away everything that was unnecessary."

At Bob Crowley's suggestion, the designer and director visited the Egyptian collection at the Metropolitan Museum of Art in New York City. They were looking for inspiration.

The opening of Aida, *in a present-day Egyptian museum (OPPOSITE) and a costume study for the scene (BELOW).*

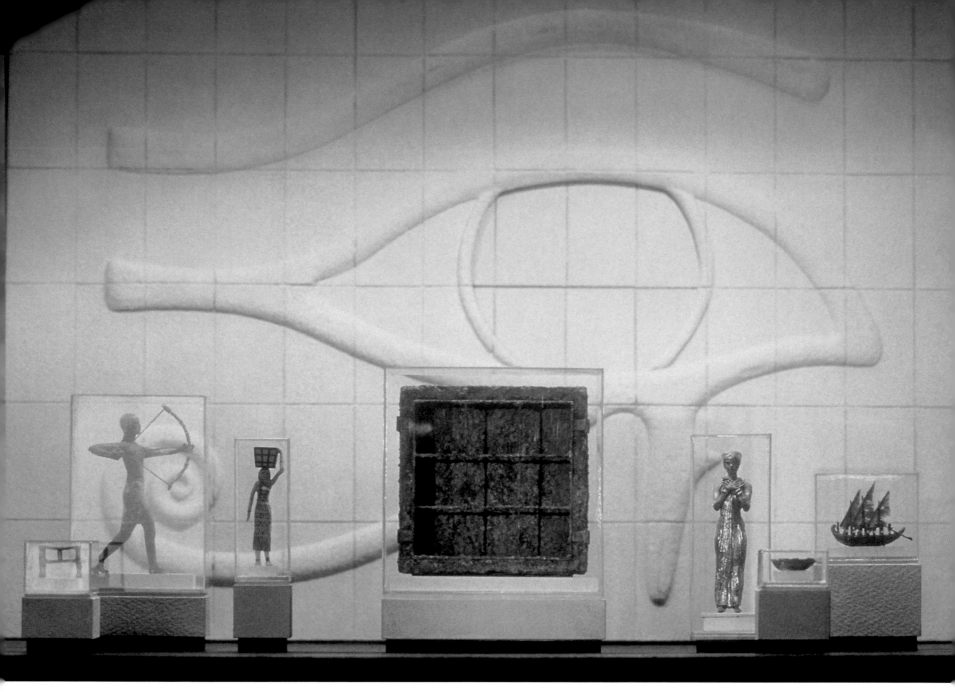

AIDA

The model for the opening
museum scene of Aida
(ABOVE) and a sketch for
the museum guard costumes
(only one was made).

"The production began to take shape after our visit to the Metropolitan Museum," designer Bob Crowley reports. He was taken by the feelings aroused by the objects that were on view there, the textures and the colors, the bleached quality of things—and the remains of intense color. "There was a purity about the Met's collection that has informed the show ever since."

There were other visual clues, too. "I'd seen this photograph of the Sphinx, where you could still see the color that is just drenched into the cheeks. I began to imagine what it must have been like when it was painted bright blue and red and green and yellow. I can't imagine how surreal that must have looked in the desert."

60

museum guard(s)

Neither of the Bobs (Crowley or Falls) wanted to replicate what they saw at the museum. They weren't looking with too literal an eye. The look of their show, they knew, would owe more to modern art and stagecraft than to archaeology. So they weren't looking for objects they could duplicate on stage. Rather, they found inspiration in the essence of what they were looking at; they were not responding to the artifacts per se, but to the feelings these pieces of an ancient puzzle have conveyed down the centuries.

Crowley went away to start his work using the "old" script, which is to say, the finished *Elaborate Lives* from the Atlanta production. Meanwhile, the script was being reworked. "Things changed a lot between my very first notions and what we wound up building," says Crowley, "but it is always great when you get off to a good start. The first conversation between the director and designer can be crucial."

It was at their initial visit to the museum that Robert Falls thought to create a modern-day frame for the ancient action of the play. When the curtain comes up on *Aida*, the audience finds itself in a white-on-white museum. The monumental blanched stone walls are carved with the pharaonic Egyptian eye of Horus. Various faded artifacts are displayed in glass cases: a ship, a vessel of some kind, a statue of a warrior complete with bow and arrow, what seems to be a standing mummy or mannequin.

The entire cast, dressed in white as modern-day museum goers, strolls through the exhibition as we begin to pick out a young woman and a young man who become more and more aware of each other and of some attraction they don't quite understand. (They are the actors who will play Aida and Radames, the roles created by Heather Headley and Adam Pascal.)

Bob Crowley costume sketches for Radames (LEFT) and Aida (ABOVE) in the museum; these modern-day costumes were not constructed but bought in a store.

Suddenly, one of the exhibits comes to life: it is the actress who plays Amneris (Sherie René Scott), and she sings the show's first song, "Every Story Is a Love Story." As the song shifts from a gentle memory to a more aggressive rock narrative, the eye of Horus opens to reveal a blazing African sun (actually an effect that mixes light and smoke and some air-blown tongues of fabric "flame"). We are transported back to ancient Nubia, where a band of women is captured by a phalanx of Egyptian soldiers. While the white world of the museum may draw its inspiration from the pale purity of

From the museum, the set changes seamlessly to Nubia (the detail is the African sun), and from Nubia to Radames' ship (the model is BELOW).

objects inherited from the past, Crowley renders the past in the bright, heavily saturated colors that adorned the objects in their own day.

Nubia is rendered by a nearly bare stage and a brilliant red backdrop. The women are captured in the course of a short dance, during which the set transforms once again: huge red triangular sails drop from the flies (the hanging space above the stage), taking us to the deck of Captain Radames' ship, and the entrance of Radames himself. It is the young man from the museum now dressed in warlike red, and boasting, in the show's next song, "Fortune Favors the Brave."

63

After a brief scene in which Aida (the young woman from the museum) shows her strength and courage—and perhaps a bit of recklessness—the stage set changes again. The fiery silk sails rise (taking two of the captain's men along with them), and the scene shifts (without a break in the action) to Radames' private chambers below decks, where Aida begins mournfully singing "The Past Is Another Land." Before she has finished, the set transforms again.

While Aida is lamenting her capture and expressing her fear of the future, the lights change, and a strange shape descends: it turns out to be a stretch of palm trees reflected along the Nile. The ship has now arrived in Egypt. This overlapping of locales means that the plot progresses seamlessly. The action does not stop for scene changes; the sets move before the ends of scenes, during scenes, propelling us forward in place as well as time.

"Design isn't just doing sets and costumes," says Bob Crowley. "It's telling a story. I'm as much involved in the transitions between one scene and the next as I am in each scene itself. You know, as a person, I am always more interested in how to get somewhere than I am in arriving. I love the journey." And with the exception of its one intermission, *Aida* is one unbroken journey from beginning to end. This almost cinematic forward motion suggests both the inevitability of everything we are seeing and its inexorability, as well. The (literally) orchestrated set changes convey the sense that we are witnessing a ritual re-enactment of something extremely important.

Because the action of the play begins in a current-day museum and switches back through the ages, the present and past become one. The production does not pretend that the actors and the audience are in Egypt in the time of the pharaohs, but acknowledges that we are in the here and now. We are seeing Egypt from our own place in the chronology of human history. So the story of ancient people can be told in modern terms without creating a tension between the way the audience perceives life and the way a culture did three or five thousand years ago. The visual elements of the production create a unity of past and present.

65

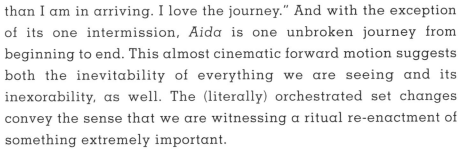

Aida (Heather Headley) in captivity in an Egypt represented by a single drop, a gangplank, and spotlight ("The Past Is Another Land," Act I).

"I like making people look at things from a slightly different perspective," explains Bob Crowley, "to distort and challenge their perceptions of the theater space, and to see things in a new way. I love the arrival into Egypt, for example, because of the way the palm trees descend upside down. They're so disconcerting the first time you see them, 'Oh, what's this thing I almost recognize? Ah, yes, they're palm trees upside down.' Like the world's turned upside down. There's a simplicity about that, and it evokes images in your own head as a member of the audience."

In fact, much of the set renders in visual terms one of the central aesthetic metaphors of the production. It is one of Robert Falls's stated objectives that all the usual elements of the musical stage come together as a single textile, a quilt that tells the story of a great doomed love. Quite on purpose, the narrative (even the exposition) is carried as much by the sets and the dances as by the book; characterizations motivate musical themes; morphing harmonies reveal evolving relationships; and the few silences of this show are as much scored and choreographed as they are directed.

And so Bob Crowley made highly inventive use of fabrics to render in gestural rather than representational terms such elements as the Nile. In one pivotal scene, Aida is given a robe of authority by her enslaved Nubian countrypeople. It is a huge piece of cloth stitched together from the scraps hoarded by this captive people. It's a ragtag royal cloak, but it serves its purpose, that of persuading Aida that she must accept her regal destiny and lead her nation out of Egypt to freedom—as Moses did the Israelites.

In another scene, slave women wash laundry against a red silk drop with the curving blue-and-white Nile painted on it. The fabric washing is choreographed, creating rhythmic flashes of blue that seem to be both cloth and water together. In the ensuing sequence, the Nile drop becomes an awning over the market-place, then Radames' tent.

In the Nubian slave camp, Aida accepts the mantle of authority from her people ("Dance of the Robe," Act I).

ABOVE: Aida and the slave women at laundry in front of the Nile drop designed by Bob Crowley (BELOW, Crowley with associate scenic designer Ted LeFevre, kneeling).

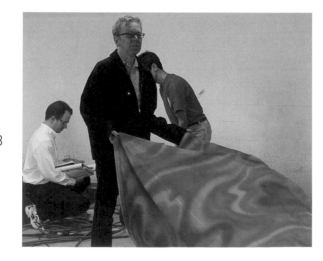

"There's a real sexiness in this story," explains Crowley, "and I wanted the world to be very sensual. To me, moving fabrics used on stage have that quality, and I've done that quite a bit. I also like things 'earning the right' to be there: that huge River Nile washing silk, you know, that suddenly gets lifted up and becomes a bazaar, and then a tent . . . That says to an audience, 'Hey, look! You know, you did this as a kid. And you haven't lost the ability to be that imaginative.' It's just that contemporary culture keeps stripping it away by making things too 'real' all the time. I wanted to do something else here, to say, 'Let's go back to the playroom and reinvent the world.'"

Crowley particularly likes the "crosscutting" of the sets as Robert Falls envisioned the scene shifts. "I love the fluidity that the camera gives you in film. I'm constantly trying to do that in the theater. I don't want to be filmic about it, because it's a contradiction in terms; I'm trying to be theatrical. But it's terrific when an actor can stand in one spot, and you can travel a thousand miles with her in the space of seconds, as when the scene shifts from Radames' boat to Egypt. I call it theater time. It's just such a magical thing to me. As a member of the audience you will go there. Aida stands there singing 'The Past Is Another Land.' She never moves, she's on that ship, and the next thing you know, she's on the docks. And you've seen it all happen, and you totally accept it. That's such a sophisticated leap of the imagination, but everybody in the house will make it.

"The great thing about Robert Falls," the designer continues, "is that he has all the references. He's got a very European sensibility when it comes to the theater because he's been running his own theater outside the commercial mainstream. So talking with him is talking on a higher level. He raises the stakes—yet we both happen to believe in giving an audience a good time."

The painted silk backdrop that forms the Nile (BELOW) becomes the bazaar canopy and then Radames' tent.

Although some designers prefer doing only costumes or sets, Crowley likes creating both. "I just think it gives a show cohesiveness—unless as a set designer you've got a fabulous relationship with the costume designer, and you think exactly the same way. There have been teams who have done that together. I haven't met that person, really, where I can just feel that they know what's inside my head. And I've found that when I don't do the clothes, I don't get to know the actors terribly well, because it's in the fittings that you connect with them, and I love actors."

Doing the sets as well as costumes also gave Crowley the opportunity to make some audacious choices, like dressing the actors entirely in reds for a scene that is also red, or dressing the court of Egypt for the banquet scene in clothing that looks more Asian than African.

In fact, the clothes have a major role to play in establishing the nonliteral, imagined world of the show. The costumes—sometimes extremely lush in color, texture, decoration, or cut (they were built by the grande dame of costume construction, Barbara Matera, and her extraordinary crew)—are as much Versace as they are Tutankhamen.

The gold costume for pharoah (OPPOSITE) was begun but not finished; the slave camp set (ABOVE) and the male banquet guest costumes (BELOW) were built as designed.

"The things we think Egyptians wore," says Crowley, "are based more on Hollywood films from the fifties, as far as I can tell, than on any authentic artifacts. But they're so familiar to us now that we run the risk of being unintentionally comic. Steve Martin puts that asp headdress on, and it's a gag. I don't know how the Egyptian culture got hijacked like that, but it did. So I thought if I had actors in little skirts and knee boots that they'd look more like Twiggy during the mod era than ancient Egyptians.

"I start from the fact that I never want an actor to look bad on stage, no matter what period it is—and some periods are better than others, some are more flattering than others. So I've given the men long coats and pants. I've looked to other cultures, too, like India, and mixed it all up a bit. Most cultures are like that anyway, all filched and borrowed and pillaged from other people, and that's what I do in the theater. And I like mixing together real things with things that are purely imaginary. It makes for a more eclectic and less literal palette. It's more important to me that the costumes have the feel or the sense of the world that's being created on stage than the look of a specific time and place."

Bob Crowley also credits more contemporary inspirations for the costumes in *Aida*, modern photography, for example, and a shop called Voyage, in London. "They started reviving that late sixties, early seventies stuff—clothes with feathers and sequins, all the hippie stuff. And I'd been looking at that, thinking it's kind of sexy. Men look great in those big baggy shirts, and those big baggy trousers, and waistcoats with beads on them. I tried to have the clothes for *Aida* read as being natural and Eastern rather than as costumes."

The sketch BELOW was a study for the women's ensemble in the River Nile scene. ABOVE: A single Egyptian soldier.

The men's ensemble as
Egyptian soldiers (ABOVE);
a working sketch for the
costumes (LEFT).

73

But each of the characters has his or her own silhouette and style. If Radames parades around in a wardrobe of vaguely Asian rock-and-roll loungewear, Princess Amneris recalls the great Hollywood movie queens. Her blue satin "spa" dress conjures Rita Hayworth in *Gilda* or Lana Turner in just about anything. And yet it feels every bit as "authentic" as the "Egyptian" costumes worn by Elizabeth Taylor in *Cleopatra*, because the costumes are meant to reveal the character, not to set a naturalistic world.

"Well, there are subtle references to Egypt in these costumes," Crowley allows, "but you've got forties glamour in there as well, which is kind of fun. As a designer, I've got to respond to the music as well as the story, and it isn't Egyptian revival music. It's Elton John pop music. So let's not get too antique about it all, let's acknowledge that it's rock and roll."

And so Chief Minister Zoser and his evil band are dressed in black, vaguely military costumes. The ensemble men's coats are built with hidden fullness in their long skirts, which flare dramatically during the "Another Pyramid" dance sequence.

Sometimes, of course, costumes have to be redesigned for comfort or for practical reasons. In the banquet sequence of Act I, for example, a trio of seemingly Indian women dances for the pharaoh. Their costumes were originally designed with long diaphanous skirts under metallic beaded belts with hundreds of tassels that went to the floor. They were time-consuming to sew, expensive, and gorgeous. But the women couldn't dance in them without getting tangled up in the beaded tassels and skirts. Everything was shortened. But what are three katakhali dancers doing in Memphis, anyway?

A costume study for the women in the bazaar scene (ABOVE); the dance costumes (BELOW) were significantly altered after they were made.

"I don't like to explain everything," designer Bob Crowley explains, "and that's what I've learned from doing Shakespeare. The minute the designer starts limiting a scene by being overly specific, by reducing the wonderful to something normal, he closes a whole series of doors into other rooms where the audience's imagination would happily wander if what they were seeing didn't stop them. So there are some scenes in *Aida* where the audience can freely imagine whatever they like. A lot of the sets are quite simple, but the stage is never totally empty. The space is always qualified by the sound or the actor or a light."

Happily for Crowley, he had lighting designer Natasha Katz to work with. They'd worked together before, on Broadway's *The Capeman* and on *Twelfth Night* at Lincoln Center.

"A bare stage is never really bare," says designer Bob Crowley, "it has actors, space, sound, and light" (a laser pyramid at RIGHT).

"I love Natasha's sensibility," says Bob Crowley, "and I love her quietness. She's a very smart woman and very sensitive."

In fact, many of the "lighting" design aspects of the show are intimately related to the set. "A lot of things are lit from within the set pieces," says Crowley, "which gives them their own energy. And I knew that we could emphasize the triangular love relationship by putting the three lovers inside a triangle of light at one point, a light that is generated by laser." By union fiat, lighting designers are also held responsible for such stage effects as fog and steam (both of which are used in *Aida*), which have to be built into the rigging plot and stage deck (the "floor" each production installs above the actual floor of the stage area).

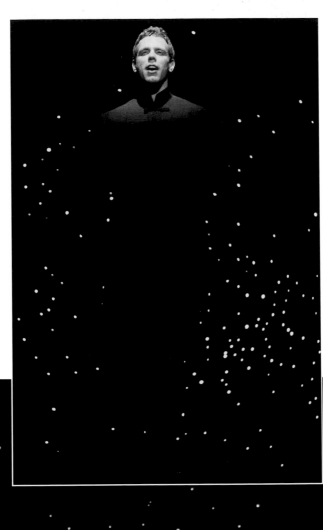

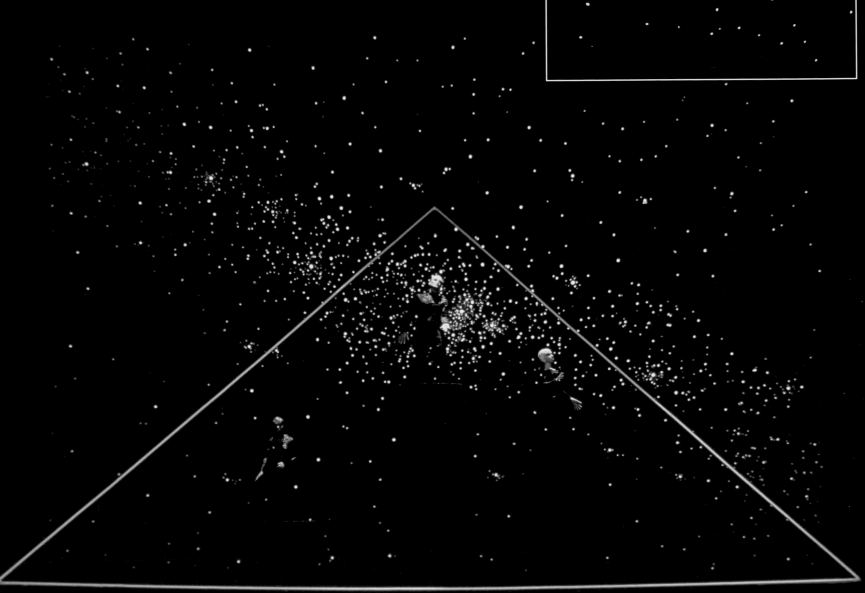

Much of lighting design is technical, "and this business has become much more technical as the years have gone by," says Natasha Katz, noting that new electronics and computers require ongoing self-education. So some of her work is technical, some very practical: "In a sense," she explains, "lighting designers are like film editors, which is to say, we're the ones who tell you where to look."

Because there is quite a bit of dancing in *Aida*, "the light plot is very dance-oriented. It's got a lot of lights on the side—a lot of low lights from the side for that very reason." Light is extremely important in dance sequences and other bare-stage sets, because light provides the mood, tone, and setting as well as the limits of vision.

But just what lights are turned on, and the qualities and colors of the light, contribute to the stage picture in poetic and subliminal as well as concrete ways. And sometimes there are compromises to make, sometimes serendipitous compromises that actually enhance the production. Katz had lit a scene in the Nubian slave camp, for example, with the extraordinarily rich colors of a memorable sunset. The scene had the clarity and color saturation of a Maxfield Parrish painting. Director Robert Falls did not see it that way.

*Aida is comforted by
a fellow Nubian slave
(Jerald Vincent) in Act II.
ABOVE: In the Nubian camp.*

"In my younger years," smiles Katz, "something like that would have bothered me, but I've learned that we're all in this process together. My job, like everyone else's, is to tell the story. So we thought it was daytime five minutes ago, and suddenly realized that the dynamic of the show is better if the scene takes place at night. That's what rehearsals are for. And I have to be able to do that without letting my ego get in the way.

"Then there's the sense that the actual time of day doesn't really matter. What the light needs to capture is not so much the literal time of day as what the characters and the audience are feeling. What we want to communicate is that the Nubians are closer to the earth than the Egyptians, so we want a more natural light on them in earthy tones. I'm not even sure how we got to the final color. It just all of a sudden appeared while I was playing with the lights—I mean, I can put any color of the rainbow up on that scrim—and it just felt like that was the right feel for a enslaved people. I mean the light really looks bruised.

79

"I'd like the banquet scene to look as if it were literally illuminated by the small hanging lamps on stage," says the lighting designer, "but the hot reds we use for the runway, for example, are not natural; they're not of the earth. So in that sequence the light takes on a very contemporary look with a very hard edge, which is appropriate to the music."

For the most part, the lighting in *Aida* is not naturalistic, and in many cases it is meant to evoke a music concert. Katz's light scheme uses banks of Vari-Lites®, the computerized tilting and rotating lights that have become a staple of the music world. "They're more in the mainstream of theater now," says Katz, "but they're an incredible tool because they have a lot of different colors and a very strong quality of light."

They are particularly effective in such big rock numbers, including those involving Zoser, Radames' scheming father. There are times during "Like Father Like Son" in Act II where Katz's lighting takes on an almost holographic quality and the set no longer looks precisely material but seems to be infused by the ethereality of the light itself, and, conversely, where the lighting seems to take on its own corporeal dimensions.

"Another Pyramid" was rechoreographed to better integrate Zoser (John Hickok) with the dancers (shown here in New York).

"Like Father Like Son"
in Chicago (Zoser's costume
was changed before the
New York opening).

FOLLOWING PAGES: *In the*
Nubian camp, Natasha Katz's
lighting adds drama to the
athletic choreography of
"Dance of the Robe."

Compounding the difficulty of the lighting plot, the multiple lighting changes are coordinated with the music.

"Well, that's the thing about a musical," Katz laughs. "We go on the five of the eight and the one of the next eight, just like the dancers. It's almost as if light and music were as closely related as dance and music. Every time I hear a modulation in the score, it's a light cue."

Aida has some 400 lighting cues. That's an average 2.6 light cues per minute, but in some places the cues come faster: there are fifty cues in the three-and-a-half-minute "Another Pyramid"— or one every 4.2 seconds.

"Lighting design is a lot like painting," Katz says. "You do what you do, and then you take a step back and look at the painting, and you go, 'Oh, I just need a little brush stroke here.' Sometimes that little brush stroke can pull the entire scene together."

81

Ironically, although *Aida* was never meant to be as large-scale or elaborate a production as Disney's *Beauty and the Beast* or *The Lion King*, getting the look of the production right was among the more difficult issues in the evolution of the show. The elements that have changed most between *Elaborate Lives* in Atlanta and *Aida* on Broadway are the script and the sets and costumes. And every change that has been made has been in the interest of streamlining and clarifying the show.

When the two Bobs first sat down to confer, they agreed on a minimalist look for the show. "We both had the same instinctive take on the piece, I think," Crowley remembers, "which was to strip it all away, starting in effect from scratch, with a blank page. And that's when we decided to go look at the Met."

But simplicity of spectacle is not necessarily easier to achieve than grandiosity. Modernist architect Mies van der Rohe might have been right that "less is more," but, as he and others have found, "less costs more," too.

"I've tried to humanize the costumes as much as I can, to simplify and pull back. I went for very simple shapes, which is one of the hardest things to do. Your design instinct is to overwork clothes so they look like you've been doing something for the last two months to justify spending so much money.

Sketches were turned into costumes at Barbara Matera's New York shop, which sometimes meant inventing new techniques.

84

Sherie René Scott is fitted for a costume she eventually wore. The labor-intensive ribbon dresses for the chorus women were replaced after Chicago.

"You're under constant pressure to make something complicated, when it comes to clothes," Bob Crowley continues. "Costume shops almost expect you to overcomplicate things." Crowley worked to reduce each scene to its essence, using colors, scale, and textures as abstract elements to communicate both the Egyptian roots and contemporary concerns of the piece. My favorite dress in the whole show is Amneris' black jersey dress for 'A Step Too Far' at the beginning of the second act."

Changes in the sets and costumes were required after the Chicago run. Crowley had designed a huge gold staircase to descend from the flies for the last scene of the first act; Pharaoh, Amneris and Radames descended from the top of the proscenium, and Amonasro, the captive Nubian king, was paraded underneath it to the great glee of Egypt. But the entire scene was cut when "The Gods Love Nubia" was moved from the second act to the Act I finale spot. The staircase, pride and joy of the set construction crew, found its way into another scene during New York previews, but eventually was jettisoned altogether, as were costumes for every member of the ensemble and such expensive props as the cage Amonasro was held in.

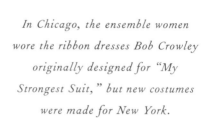

*In Chicago, the ensemble women
wore the ribbon dresses Bob Crowley
originally designed for "My
Strongest Suit," but new costumes
were made for New York.*

But as sets go, so do they come. An entire new scene—the map room—was written for the production between Chicago and New York. That meant a new costume for Amneris, who appears in the scene. The bold word *NUBIA*, which had once stretched across the stage during the opening of the show, was cut because it seemed extraneous. A silk drop that had been painted with Japanese-style waves was also deleted as unnecessary.

Changes in the runway sequence after Chicago required changes in both the sets and costumes. Crowley had designed dresses for Amneris and her handmaidens of woven ribbons, and then added wild hats with Egyptian themes. But, it was agreed, the ensemble women needed individualized dresses. Six new dresses were made for the handmaidens, a not inconsiderable expense. Adjustments to the electric closet wall had to be made, too, to accommodate changes in the choreography.

Some changes were made for other than aesthetic reasons. The tomb in which Radames and Aida are buried was designed to rise off the stage deck in the dark. But the machinery that was holding up the tomb gave way at a Chicago preview, injuring Heather Headley and Adam Pascal, who fell with the set piece in front of a horrified full house at Chicago's Palace Theatre. It was decided for the sake of safety and security that the tomb would remain on the ground.

86

OPPOSITE: *Heather Headley and Sherie René Scott have appeared as Aida and Amneris in Atlanta, Chicago, and New York—in a steadily evolving sequence of costumes and wigs.*

ABOVE: *Amneris' closet, in model and on stage.* BELOW: *The "light rods" in "Like Father Like Son" were replaced by metal ones.*

Every change in the set or costumes, in the choreography or the book scenes of the show, of course, meant changes in the lighting: additions, deletions, alterations. The "light rods," expensive props that behaved skittishly and hamstrung the choreography of "Like Father Like Son," were replaced by the metal rods used in New York.

"Well," says Bob Crowley philosophically, "the most important thing is telling the story. You don't want to distract from that. I believe that you should give an audience a really good time, as well. There's a huge responsibility inherent in doing a show like this. People pay a lot of money now to go and see these things. And there are certain expectations you have to consider. You can't pretend they don't exist. You have to deliver what people came to the theater to see.

"Now, you can tell a great and serious story with some measure of the old Broadway razzmatazz. And you can also hold back and say, 'Look, actually, I'm not going to do anything here now. We'll just have an actor singing a song in a beautiful space in nice lighting.' If there's always a whole lot of scenery on stage," suggests Crowley, "it can exhaust an audience. There's a law of diminishing returns, you know. There is such a thing as too much."

When all the changes were made, the juxtapositions of these razzmatazz and bare-stage scenes work to keep the entire experience of *Aida* in balance and the emotional through-line in focus.

"AND WHO'D HAVE THOUGHT THAT LOVE COULD BE SO GOOD?

NOT ME, NOT ME ...,

AND SHOW ME THINGS I NEVER UNDERSTOOD,

NOT ME ...NOT ME ...."

From "Not Me" by Elton John and Tim Rice

CHAPTER FOUR
PERFORMANCE

"AS A DIRECTOR," Robert Falls summarizes, "you see something in your head. You see it and hear it. When you direct, you're trying to match what you are doing to that inner vision. But you also have to be open to things you don't hear. The real challenge for a director is to have a strong vision, to guide it along to the place it needs to be guided—but also to be open to other ideas."

In creating the show, in "putting it up on its feet," Falls had at his disposal his cast, his orchestra, and collaborators Wayne Cilento, as choreographer, and Paul Bogaev as musical director and music producer (not to mention associates, assistants, and others.

"The first time we met," says Wayne Cilento of his initial meeting with Robert Falls, "I don't think we spoke much about the show at all. We were just kind of feeling out each other's vibe.

"When we did start talking about the show what I said was that I thought I could create the life around these three characters with movement. I could make this world come alive by tapping into all kinds of stylistic dancing—East Indian and African, for example. But because *Aida* is a rock or pop score, I'd have the liberty to mix in something as contemporary as "Another Pyramid," which is the MTV video kind of approach, because a number like that should help give the show a contemporary edge. From the beginning everyone seemed to be on the same wavelength."

The ensemble during the first New York run-through prior to Chicago. BELOW (seated from left): Bob Crowley, Thomas Schumacher, Elton John, Robert Falls, and (standing) Paul Bogaev and choreographer Wayne Cilento.

The collaborative nature of the project was also appealing to Cilento. "I'm not interested in going into a room to make dance steps to insert into a piece. I want to be involved with the process. I want to offer something through body language that basically enhances, and keeps telling, the story. So, it's not like, 'Okay, here comes the dance entertainment; okay, now they're gone, let's get on with the story.'"

Throughout their working relationship, Falls and Cilento worked to integrate the dance with the action of *Aida*. Almost every change that was made to the choreography in rehearsals for Chicago and again for New York was designed to tie all the elements together in a more and more cohesive whole. In fact, during tech rehearsals in Chicago and New York, it was often Cilento who worked with lighting designer Natasha Katz to focus and hone the lighting.

OPPOSITE: John Hickok as Zoser in "Like Father Like Son" in Chicago; THIS PAGE: The men in the ensemble rehearse their two numbers as Zoser's henchmen in New York.

"Wayne took the lead on the musical numbers, and I worked with Natasha on the nonmusical scenes," says Robert Falls, "and then we'd all sort it out together. In a working collaboration, the creative impulse is carried by different people. I'd hand it off to Wayne, and then he'd throw it back to me, or forward it to Paul Bogaev." Occasionally there were other collaborators, as well. Fight director Rick Sordelet worked with Cilento to stage the "Like Father Like Son" number in Act II, for example, and with Robert Falls in staging Aida's swordplay in her first scene.

"Bob Falls is very secure in what he is as a director," says Wayne Cilento, "and I'm very secure in who I am as a choreographer. What I was excited about doing was offering my life experience as a dancer, choreographer, and director to this show to help create something fresh, something new. In the course of working, I'd sometimes worry that I was overstepping my boundaries and pull back. I'd go to Bob and say, 'What do you think about this?' And he'd say, 'Go do it.'"

95

Choreographer Wayne Cilento
plays to his dancers' strengths.
THESE PAGES: *The nine men*
in the ensemble as
Zoser's henchmen.

96

"Well," says Falls, "one person ultimately steps up and takes control. And it's the director whose job is to be the ultimate arbitrator. It's like the general of an army—even though it's an over-used metaphor. It does feel like you're running an army when you're overseeing a production on this scale. But Wayne and I worked very closely together. For example, we always knew that "Another Pyramid" would take place on a bare stage, and it was going to be just music, movement, and lights. So it required a real collaboration between Wayne, Natasha, and Paul. During tech rehearsals, it made sense for them to work out the details. And then I'd just chime in when I saw something I didn't think was working dramatically."

"A lighting designer needs to feel the music and know where I'm going," says Cilento, "both in the individual number and in the progression of the show. When I make an emotional adjustment in the movement, the lights need to make an emotional adjustment, or you lose that 'in sync' quality, and that can really hurt a number. That's why it was so great to work with Natasha Katz, who gets it all.

"I think 'Another Pyramid' is a perfect example of a collaboration of choreography, music, costumes, and lights," Cilento continues. "Because the dream is to have that movement with those men and have it be strong, to have the flow and the physicality of it match what Bob Crowley's jackets are doing and Natasha's lighting is doing."

In Cilento's case, he was also collaborating with his dancers—right from the auditions, part of which he conducted with sequences he'd already worked out for the show. "Auditioning is such a dreadful experience," says a man who knows from experience. "It's devastating. So, I always try to make an audition a growing and learning experience. If you get the show, great; if you don't, you walk out of the room and think, 'That was an incredible experience. I had a great time. I don't care if I get the job.'"

The choreography includes moments of individuation and others of unified movement, all cued to changes in the lighting as well as to the music.

97

"I learned a lot from watching Wayne's auditions," says Robert Falls. "You could sit there hour after hour and see which of the dancers really shone, which ones really took to his brand of choreography. In rehearsals, he really draws on the strengths of his individuals, featuring whatever they do well. So everybody is dancing at the top of their ability."

Throughout rehearsals, the *Aida* ensemble dancers (which included only four dancers from the Atlanta *Elaborate Lives* run) were effusive in their affection for and dedication to Cilento, an energy field who draws creative life forms into his orbit.

"I've wanted to work with Wayne ever since I saw *Tommy*," says ensemble member Eric Sciotto, who appeared previously on Broadway with Bernadette Peters in *Annie Get Your Gun*. "Wayne likes things to come out of you organically, and that lets you put your own signature and personality onto things. And it's particularly exciting when you're originating a show, because as a dancer you're helping to create it. He makes us work our tails off, but we want to do that for him, because he works so hard for us."

"Well, I think when you're creating a new show you're building it around specific people who each have something unique to offer, which is why casting is so important," says Cilento. "I do a lot of preparation for a show, and I'm very specific about what I want a lot of the time. But there are sections where I need to tap into what people do the best.

"So there are passages where I would say there's been some improvisation, or at least exploration. If I need a high moment at a certain point in the score, I may not particularly care exactly what the move is. I know someone has to jump on the count of five and I want it pretty up there, but I don't really know what I want the dancer to do until I see what he or she is good at. Then I take what they do and set it."

The choreography in "Another Pyramid" and in the runway segment of "My Strongest Suit" are, perhaps, the dance numbers most influenced by the individual dancers. Changes in the runway orchestration and costumes between Chicago and New York required some changes in the choreography. The order in which the women take to the runway is in part dictated by how long it takes each one to make her quick change, and even that affects the choreography.

In working out the runway sequence, Wayne Cilento gave the women some latitude for improvisation in the process. OPPOSITE: Youn Kim.

Of course, all this individuation makes it tough on understudies and swings. When the show opened, *Aida* had four swing dancers, two men and two women, who covered all the male and female ensemble roles. That meant as many as eight different harmonies in the songs and as many roles in the dances, and the swings often didn't know until they showed up at the theater which role they would play for that performance, if any.

"Wayne does not have any two women doing the same thing at any time," jokes swing dancer Kelli Fournier. "Maybe one count of eight in the whole show. Every day I watch one woman and write down her charts and then I go home and try to learn the moves."

"We have got great dancers in this show," boasts their choreographer. "The swings are brilliant. I've got to say that it's probably the hardest job you can possibly do. But if you get into it, and you do it successfully, it's got to be the most rewarding as well as the most challenging."

While it may seem fairly straightforward to take a completed Broadway show score and put it up on stage, the process is far more complex. In the case of *Aida*, the songs themselves changed very little after they were written. However, some songs moved from the first act to the second, and vice versa; others were assigned to different characters, given new lyrics to convey different meanings or were reconceived as duets, trios, or quartets. One song, "The Messenger," a particular favorite of the composer, was deleted from the show after Atlanta.

"I'm sad that 'The Messenger' is gone," admits Elton John, "but that's a directorial decision. I was told that introducing a new song after Aida and Radames were in the tomb was just too jarring, that the audience wasn't with it. So I bow to the people who know better."

In the big meeting at the end of the Chicago run, Bob Falls had the idea that "Elaborate Lives" should be sung not by Aida to Radames, but by Radames to Aida. It was a wrenching idea for everyone at first. "Elton took some convincing," Falls reports, but when you're working in uncharted territory, every available road that presents itself has to be explored to see if, indeed, it's the one you are searching for."

The women's ensemble rehearses "My Strongest Suit" in New York in November 1999 (OPPOSITE) and performs it on Broadway in March 2000 (ABOVE).

101

For one thing, reassigning "Elaborate Lives" meant it had to be reconsidered musically for a different actor singing the song in a voice with different inherent characteristics. "Every song in the score," says music director Bogaev, "was explored for the individual actor in a specific moment in the production."

"It was a bit traumatic," says Robert Falls, "because we all loved the way Heather sang it. But the love story needed the song to come from Radames."

"It was like somebody took my child away," Heather Headley admits.

PRECEDING PAGES:
The Nubian slaves in "Dance
of the Robe"—dancers moving
through space and light.

THIS PAGE: Radames and
Aida are entombed together,
but pledge eternal love, in
performance on the ground
(LEFT) and as originally
conceived, up in the air (ABOVE).

"Speaking selfishly," says Adam Pascal in his dressing room before the last New York preview with makeup supervisor Jorge Vargas applying his "eye of Horus" tattoo, "it was good for me and for Radames, because it's a great, great song. But it was really difficult to sing it to Heather because she sang it so magnificently. And I knew she was unhappy not to be singing it, and I was unhappy because I loved listening to her singing it."

"I did not want to make that change at first," says Headley, "but I had to ask myself, 'Is this my ego talking, or is this me wanting the best for the show?' So Adam and I talked it over, because it was uncomfortable for him, as well. But when it was decided to reprise the song, to bring it back at the end of Act II, it was as if we could share custody of the child. The truth is that I enjoy singing it more where it is now than where it was before, because I love it more."

105

A second song, "Our Nation Holds Sway," which had been a theme song for Radames and the Egyptian warriors, was thought too generic after Chicago. "Well, it was never much of a song," says Aida's lyricist, Tim Rice. "It was kind of cobbled together from some themes Elton wrote and some lyrics I wrote for the scene." Giving Radames a stronger entrance was one of the changes to be made before opening in New York.

"We just felt we needed something a bit more structured, perhaps," says Rice. "And we wanted to say something a bit different. Emotionally, it fills the same arc between two songs that have remained the same: 'Every Story Is a Love Story,' from the prologue, and Aida's 'The Past Is Another Land.'

"Fortune Favors the Brave": Elton John and Tim Rice wrote a new song after Chicago to introduce the character of Radames (Adam Pascal performs it on Broadway, ABOVE).

"It's interesting about the day-to-day process of working a musical," Tim Rice continues, "and it was the same on this show as it has been on others I've worked on: You always have to change some lyrics as the book evolves. But for *Aida*, I'd say ninety percent of the lyrics have never changed. There are always one or two lyrics such that once you change them, you wind up changing them five times. Most of the songs in this show have not had a word changed since they were written, 'Easy as Life,' for example."

Most, however, did do a lot of traveling in the course of the rehearsal period, from one act to the other, from one place within the act to another, from one actor to another. Sometimes a song moved several times before finding its best place in the score.

"Frankly," admits Sir Tim, "I resist change wherever I can, because rewriting one lyric can tumble a whole house of cards."

"The words and the melody are only the skeleton of what the actors have to learn," says veteran music director Paul Bogaev, whose Broadway credits have included *Sunset Boulevard* with Glenn Close and *Les Misérables*, among many others. "Then we all take each song apart and work it until we get the right tone for the song, for the scene, and for the show."

By "we all," Bogaev refers to a musical team that includes Elton John, Tim Rice, and Guy Babylon, who is Elton John's keyboardist and who created some of *Aida*'s arrangements and orchestrations. Also on the staff were orchestrator Steve Margoshes, arrangers Bob Gustafson, Jim Abbott, and Gary Seligson, and music coordinator Michael Keller.

Guy Babylon, who served as a kind of resident "Elton expert," has been John's keyboard player for a dozen years, and has been involved in *Aida* since its inception. "I was with Elton when he wrote the tunes," says Babylon. "He would give me an idea of what direction he wanted the song to go in, and I would do my best right on the spot to give it some shape and direction. He'd say, 'I want this up-tempo, I want a ballad, I want this reggae, whatever.' And then I'd give him a tempo or a drum machine pattern to write to. Then he'd write the melody and the chords, and lay down the lyric. Some of the songs have changed a great deal since we first conceived them, but others have changed very little."

Choreographer Wayne Cilento working on "Elaborate Lives" with Heather Headley and Adam Pascal.

107

Like all people who come together to work on a single project, this creative team had to negotiate its working relationships. "At the beginning," says Adam Pascal, "Paul Bogaev was concerned with certain things being very precise, but I don't sing that way. I don't even read music. So he needed to relax a little bit and let Heather and Sherie and me sort of suss out how we were going to sing together and just let it evolve.

"Bob Falls," Pascal continues, "really just kind of lets you go. If you're straying too far from where he wants you, he'll nudge you back. But he doesn't say, 'Okay, this is what this is, and I want you to do it like that.' He really lets you run with it, which is liberating."

"I know some people think that film is the most collaborative art form," says Sherie René Scott, "but it's not true. Nothing requires more creativity than musical theater. I mean, it's not like, the score is done now so we'll add the songs and dances. There's a constant state of barely controlled chaos because everything is evolving at the same time and sometimes at a furious pace."

One of Radames' songs had been problematic since Atlanta. "We weren't sure that 'Enchantment Passing Through' was going

to work," says Paul Bogaev in preparing the show for Chicago. "It came at a place of particular anger for the character, but the song has an inherent sweetness to it. So we pushed the song as far as we could without breaking it. What we wound up with was very spare, something you might not immediately think is appropriate for the song, but it's much more interesting for the character in that moment, and it works for Adam, who has to sing it."

In fact, "Enchantment Passing Through" was rethought again between Chicago and New York, as a duet for Radames and Aida. It gave the pair a private scene after the public announcement of Radames' forthcoming marriage to Amneris. Alone together, the two ill-fated lovers can explore the things they begin to love about each other.

Elton John makes a vocal point (ABOVE) during rehearsals. As the three main characters explored their relationships, the words, movements, even songs were changed.

109

"Paul Bogaev knows how he wants a song to sound," says Adam Pascal, who tore onto the Broadway scene in *Rent*, the AIDS-era retelling of *La Bohème*, "but he was open to us putting our own flavors on the songs. I mean, this is me singing, not Elton John, and even Elton doesn't sing his own songs the same way twice."

Certainly the composer was not trying to impose the sound of his voice on his cast. "I've never told them how to sing a song," says Elton John, "I said, 'Just put yourself into it.' And I've never had cause to say, 'You're not doing it right.' I've spoken to them in rehearsal and said, 'You can ease up on this a little," but nothing major. I had to be careful not to Elton-ize them too much. And that was hard, because I have a certain style. But these lead actors sing these songs beautifully."

"Part of my job," says Paul Bogaev, "is to render Elton's songs in theatrical terms. I certainly don't believe in changing melodies. Elton is a great composer of vocal music, and I don't mess with that. *Aida* is meant to be something between a musical and a concert, but it's not only a concert, with one song after another. Each song is part of a narrative whole, and the score needs a unity that a concert doesn't. So the East Indian themes from the banquet dance theme crop up elsewhere, too, for example.

"To get that integration, we've used all kinds of strategies. We've done orchestrations that that use variations of one song as accompaniment to another. Or we'll vary things subtly from the way they were written to suit the emotional content of a scene. We thinned out the chord structure of "The Past Is Another Land" so it wasn't as pretty a ballad as it had been originally written.

"At one point in the process we actually combined two songs that had not been written to be sung together, 'Not Me' and 'Elaborate Lives.' And it sounded great as a trio, but ultimately it was decided that the end of the show was dragging, that is was becoming too much song/scene/song/scene. So a whole sequence was reduced to a few lines, and the double reprise was eliminated."

A week before the New York opening, Elton John took issue with the orchestrations of the runway scene, which he felt strayed too far into techno-pop. The sequence was reorchestrated several ways, including retro-disco. It appears in the show with a more classic rock orchestration.

Actors Heather Headley and Adam Pascal had to go deep to discover why Aida and Radames would ever fall in love.

The music in today's Broadway musicals is tied in performance to sound technology, and that creates a new level of problems along with new solutions, but there are many complex considerations. "There are obvious things," says sound designer Steve C. Kennedy, "like the size and nature of the venue, and whether it's a rock show or a more orchestral score, like *Titanic*.

"But everything that makes a sound plays into it," says sound associate John Shivers. "The specific orchestrations, the number of actors, the specific instrumentations not only affect the way we shape the sound, but what equipment we use, from the console to the speakers." For *Aida* most of the performers' microphones are built into hair designer David Brian Brown's wigs. That meant creating a wig for Heather Headley (whose real hair is cropped far too short to hide a microphone).

Every change in the score requires reprogramming the sound as well as the lights. If more of a film winds up on the cutting-room floor than on screen, it is also true that more of a Broadway musical is left in rehearsal halls and on the road than ever appears in the environs of Times Square.

"Yes," sighs Paul Bogaev, "it's difficult to work hard on something and have it cut or changed. But that's the job: to tell the story. The music staff kept writing and rewriting throughout the rehearsal process, and there was a constant back-and-forth between us and Elton."

"I can't say enough about Elton John as a collaborative spirit," says director Robert Falls. "Elton is so comfortable with himself and his gifts, has such confidence in his score that he relies on and listens to the other collaborators. He lets us do the things he does not necessarily know how to do."

Of course, if John doesn't like the way something is going, he isn't shy about saying so. Word may come by way of phone, fax, or E-mail, or by a visit to the rehearsal hall (sometimes in casual sports gear, sometimes in sophisticated designer ensembles). One particular day John took issue with the backup rhythms on "My Strongest Suit." Popping up from his seat, he went to the piano and started hammering out his own ideas, singing the women's vocal lines and going so far as to teach them the quicker cadences he had in mind."

The "Dance of the Robe" scene in Act I is a fusion of acting, music, dance, and visual spectacle (set, costumes, light).

113

"Elton just had a real sense of how he wanted to change it," Falls says of that particular spontaneous moment, "and he wanted to work on it. So I let him."

That kind of electricity has not been unusual in the process of bringing this new *Aida* to the stage. "Everyone is so talented," says Heather Headley. "We have just been in awe of each other right from the beginning," she adds. "The way people put their talent to work inspires enormous respect, so everyone, from Elton and Tim to Bob and Wayne and Paul, is open to our input as actors. It makes people feel valued, so everyone is working at their best. It's really inspirational. And that's what makes it possible to make a change that hurts."

"I always look to the chorus as the real barometer of what's going on in the rehearsal process," says Sherie René Scott, who originates the role of Amneris. "And they feel like valued actors in the process, not just bodies. They have characters and actions in each scene and have had a lot of creative input. And that helps everyone."

But even the ensemble members have to adjust to changes. Two entire dance routines were cut from the show between Chicago and New York, two numbers to which hundreds of rehearsal hours had been devoted. "And every time there's a change in a number," jokes swing dancer Chris Payne Dupré, "I have to learn eight new tracks."

"Right from Atlanta, we all had to keep asking ourselves, 'What is best for the show?'" says Heather Headley in her dressing room shortly before opening night. "You know we performers like to have our moments. And it was sometimes hard for me when Bob Falls would come to me and say, 'Cut that'—because I have built that moment into the through-line of my performance. But if the director says that your moment is holding up the show or distracting the

"The Gods Love Nubia," the Act I finale on Broadway (ABOVE) was in the second act in Chicago.

114

audience from the action, I have to trust him and do what he says. I certainly have to try whatever he suggests and to make it work."

And occasionally things change back. "Well, that makes me feel confident that I know what I'm doing," Headley laughs. "I love hearing the director say, 'You were right, let's do it your way.'"

The relationships between and among Headley, Scott, and Pascal are part of what holds *Aida* together as a show. The three actors have been fiercely supportive of each other ever since they started working together.

"I've worked with a lot of talented people," says Sherie René Scott, "but Adam and Heather still stun me—literally. And that's every show. I get to where I just have to shake my head because

Even in the spoken scenes, movement is choreographed. Radames pursues a flirtatious Aida (BELOW).

it's so unbelievable to me what they're able to do eight times a week. And the vocal consistency they have, and their ability to stay present, alive, honest, and still to sing like no one has sung on Broadway in years. I know there are a lot of beautiful voices out there, but these two can do anything."

The mutual support made the process of continued exploration easier. "Each time we had to go back and consider the character relationships," the actress continues, "I had to stay open to the other two. After Atlanta, after Chicago, the point was to figure out the triangle, to find the moments of connection and provide the motivations for the deep, deep love these people share, all the different levels of love. And what was great was that everyone came in each time, each day and stayed open-minded. And because we all came to trust each other so much, we felt safe enough to really feel our own feelings, thoughts, and feelings that contribute to the creative process and actually help the others."

115

Adam Pascal, originating the role of Radames, was new to the cast after Atlanta and thinks he's had the easier time by joining the project when he did. "I think everyone always knew where the character of Radames needed to be," he says, "but it was a long process getting there, and that character was reconceived after Atlanta. I think it would have been more difficult for me to have played the character and then had to rethink it for a different production. And because the three of us are so intimately connected, a change in any of our parts changes the whole dynamic of the show. So, you can't just change one of the characters, you have to change them all."

Even in Chicago the cast knew there was still room to grow. "I thought that Radames was more a facilitator for Aida than a fully realized character of his own," says Adam Pascal. "He wasn't interesting enough. There was no reason for Aida to fall in love with him. I mean, he's the enemy!

"So we had to make it clear that there are things in him that are innately good. That's what makes him different from his father. Yes, he took the women captive, but he saves them from the copper mines. There's passion in him: he's an explorer, but there's something missing from him. I think that's why he's so in love with exploration and discovery. And what he finds in her is ultimately what's missing in him. She is everything that he wants to be. What he's really looking for is himself—and Aida gives him that."

"To me," says Sherie René Scott, "Amneris was always a misunderstood woman, a misunderstood girl, and I think a lot of women can identify with that. The trick was to make her a misunderstood person with a lot of depth, a woman who is not adequately seen. And that's why she is so vulnerable to Aida, who understands her immediately. The role doesn't work if she's too funny all the way through the show. Then the audience writes her off as superficial, too.

"What's exciting for me now is that I really feel Amneris embodies some sort of essence of femaleness that a lot of women can identify with, that we have to hide our light, to hide our strength. And we cover it with superficial things that distract us and others from our true potential and our true power," the actress continues.

"Elaborate Lives": Adam Pascal and Heather Headley make it look easy and natural, but every gesture and expression has been worked out and set.

117

"You know," adds Sherie René Scott, "Amneris is like Marilyn Monroe or Princess Diana—they fell into the trap anyone can fall into to be loved. I think that contributes to why people are moved by this show, because Amneris is on a journey that all women have to take. And that's what's been fun, to fully realize the arc of this character. Plus, the humor is great. People love it so much, and humor is a sign of intelligence."

"Aida has definitely changed over the last three years," says Heather Headley of the character she says she loves. "I was thinking the other day that just as she's matured in the process of discovering the play, I've also grown up. And I think—and pray—that the changes are good for us both. Because both of us had to step back from ourselves to look at a bigger picture. I had to find the things in myself that would make a princess fall in love with her captor."

"Well," says bookwriter David Henry Hwang, "that was the crucial issue. We had to provide the cues not only for the characters but for the audience, too. The rehearsal process was sometimes kind of heavy. We kept coming back to the question, 'What would make a woman in a concentration camp fall in love with a Nazi guard?' Because that actually happened. And if that could happen, we could find the reasons in Radames and Aida that they could fall in love."

"Look," concedes Adam Pascal, "it was difficult. It was a challenge. It was a frustrating process— and it was wonderful all at the same time. It was hard, and very, very good. The payoff is that I think the show's in a place that I'm proud of. You know, you make a decision to take a job, and you wind up with a new family. I love Sherie and Heather. The three of us have a very special relationship. I think they're truly princesses. But I love everyone in the cast."

"I love these people," agrees Sherie René Scott, "and I love this show. I mean this is a complex story

120

PRECEDING PAGES:
Deep emotions rendered
simply: Zoser foils the escape
plot, Mereb dies, Aida and
Radames are captured.

Amneris in transformation
from spoiled princess to
Queen of Egypt (with Daniel
Oreskes as Pharaoh, LEFT).

that has evolved from a very brief outline. The long creative process we've been through from the beginning has added a deep spirituality to the piece. *Aida* becomes a statement about forgiveness and about loyalty and about true love. It's about people changing."

"This show moves people," says Heather Headley—which has been true of *Aida* since the early workshops of the play. "It's my joy as a performer to be in a show that's about something, that moves people to break down or cry. I want the audiences' toes to be involved on this one. I want them to enjoy themselves, but I am also incredibly gratified by having people say to me, 'I was so touched, and my life was changed,' and people have said those things to me. I believe that theater can change the way people look at things, can make them better people. I know *Aida* can."

Amneris (Sherie René Scott) is dressed for a long-awaited but no longer joyous marriage to Radames.

121

EPILOGUE

"I'M SO TIRED OF ALL WE'RE GOING THROUGH
I DON'T WANT TO LIVE LIKE THAT
I JUST WANT TO BE WITH YOU
NOW AND FOREVER, PEACEFUL...TRUE..."

From "Elaborate Lives" by Elton John and Tim Rice

FINALLY, AIDA AND RADAMES are condemned to die for conspiring in the escape of the captured king of Nubia, Aida's father. They will be buried alive beneath the sands of Egypt. Amneris, made strong by her despair, claims her right to inherit the throne from her ailing father, and demands that the two people she loves most be buried in the same tomb.

As they enter it, we realize that it is the same mysterious object we saw in the museum scene that opens the production. Aida and Radames pledge their eternal love. They vow to look for one another, if necessary, for a hundred lifetimes.

The lights dim. The music swells. A new star twinkles in the sky, and the story of Aida and Radames is over....

But *Aida* is not, not quite.

Just as the play begins in the present, the action returns to the present, to the Egyptian museum, where the same people we saw some two and a half hours earlier are reenacting the scene. We realize that the two young people who had been drawn mysteriously to each other at the beginning of the play are the reincarnations of Aida and Radames. They have found each other, after a hundred lifetimes, in a better time and place, where their love is not forbidden or impossible.

The modern-day Radames and the modern-day Aida move toward one another with a sense of adventure and discovery as... the curtain closes.

Love has conquered death.

THIS PAGE AND PRECEDING PAGES: The last scene of Aida *repeats the first, but everything has changed.*

The End

HYPERION THEATRICALS
under the direction of
Peter Schneider and Thomas Schumacher
presents

A I D A

Music by
ELTON JOHN

Lyrics by
TIM RICE

Book by
LINDA WOOLVERTON
and
ROBERT FALLS & DAVID HENRY HWANG

SUGGESTED BY THE OPERA

Original Cast

**HEATHER HEADLEY   ADAM PASCAL   SHERIE RENÉ SCOTT
JOHN HICKOK   DAMIAN PERKINS
TYREES ALLEN   DANIEL ORESKES**

ROBERT M. ARMITAGE   NEIL BENARI   TROY ALLAN BURGESS   FRANNE CALMA
CHRIS PAYNE DUPRÉ   THURSDAY FARRAR   KELLI FOURNIER   BOB GAYNOR
KISHA HOWARD   TIM HUNTER   YOUN KIM   KYRA LITTLE   KENYA UNIQUE MASSEY
CORINNE McFADDEN   PHINEAS NEWBORN III   JODY RIPPLINGER   RAYMOND RODRIGUEZ
ERIC SCIOTTO   TIMOTHY EDWARD SMITH   ENDALYN TAYLOR-SHELLMAN
SAMUEL N. THIAM   JERALD VINCENT   SCHELE WILLIAMS   NATALIA ZISA

Scenic & Costume Design
BOB CROWLEY

Lighting Design
NATASHA KATZ

Sound Design
STEVE C. KENNEDY

Hair Design
DAVID BRIAN BROWN

Makeup Design
NAOMI DONNE

Music Produced and
Musical Direction by
PAUL BOGAEV

Music Arrangements
**GUY BABYLON
PAUL BOGAEV**

Orchestrations
**STEVE MARGOSHES
GUY BABYLON
PAUL BOGAEV**

Music Coordinator
MICHAEL KELLER

Dance Arrangements
**BOB GUSTAFSON
JIM ABBOTT
GARY SELIGSON**

Technical Supervision
THEATERSMITH, INC.

Development Casting
JAY BINDER

Casting
BERNARD TELSEY

Flight Direction
RICK SORDELET

Associate Producer
MARSHALL B. PURDY

Press Representative
BONEAU/BRYAN-BROWN

Production Supervisor
CLIFFORD SCHWARTZ

Choreography by
WAYNE CILENTO

Directed by
ROBERT FALLS

Hyperion Theatricals

Peter Schneider   Thomas Schumacher
Producers

Creative Affairs .... Stuart Oken
General Manager .... Alan Levey
Physical Production .... John De Santis
Executive Music Producer ..... Chris Montan
Business Affairs .... Kevin Breen,
    Gabrielle Klatsky, Robbin Kelley,
    Harry S. Gold, Raymond Wu,
    Karen Lewis
Labor Relations .... John Petrafesa, Sr.,
    Robert W. Johnson, Leslie Ann Bennett
Marketing .... Lisa Kitei, Ron Kollen,
    Carol Chiavetta, Jack Eldon,
    Andrew Flatt, Fiona Thomas,
    Todd Wingfield, John Wood
Group Sales .... Jacob Lloyd Kimbro
Development .... Michelle Mindlin
Finance .... Jeff Farnath,
    Amy Copeland, David Schrader,
    Saundra Berry, Patricia Busby,
    Pauline Callender, Jamie Cousins,
    Jason Fletcher, Steven Guilbaud,
    Steven Klein, Alex Lerner,
    Joe McClafferty, Danielle Pinnt,
    Regina Spencer, Bradley Stephens,
    Jennifer Stevens
Box Office Operations .... Jerome Kane
Theatre Management/Operations ....
    .... Dana Amendola
Production Supervisors .... Bob Routolo,
    John Tiggeloven
Staff Associate Designer ....
    .... Dennis W. Moyes
Administrative Staff .... Elliot Altman,
    Leslie Barrett, Philip Geoffrey Bond,
    Kevin Boyer, Tami Carlson,
    Stephanie Cheek, Jennifer Clark,
    Kevin Cordova, Chris Diamond,
    Carl Flanigan, Joel Hile,
    Jay Hollenbeck, Debbie Hoy,
    Stacie Iverson, Connie Jasper,
    Lisa Kudry, Antonia Law,
    Aaron Levin, Lisa Majewski,
    Diane Mellen, Kelli Palan,
    Sharon Petti, Lawrence Pfeil,
    Andrea Prince, Doug Quandt,
    Roberta Risafi, Royal Riedinger,
    Robyn Ruehl, Chesley Seals,
    Susan Tyker, Marianne Virtuoso,
    Pam Waterman, Julianna Wineland

Staff for *Aida*

Project Manager .... Ken Silverman
Assistant to the Associate Producer ....
    .... Lisa Edwards
Production Accountant .... Bill Hussey

Associate Director .... KEITH BATTEN
Associate Choreographer ....
    .... TRACY LANGRAN COREA

General Press Representative
BONEAU/BRYAN-BROWN
Chris Boneau,   Jackie Green,   Steven Padla

COMPANY MANAGER ....
.... MICHAEL SANFILIPPO
Assistant Company Manager ....
.... Lisa Koch

Stage Manager .... Paul J. Smith
Assistant Stage Managers ....
.... Caroline Ranald Curvan,
    Valerie Lau-Kee Lai
Assistant Director .... Hilary Adams
Dance Captain .... Jody Ripplinger
Assistant Dance Captain ....
.... Timothy Edward Smith
Fight Captain .... Raymond Rodriguez

Associate Scenic Designer ...... Ted LeFevre
Scenic Design Assistants ...... Mike Britton,
    Dan Kuchar
Drafting .... Jane Mancini, Paula Sjoblorn
Modelbuilders .... Hyun-Joo Kim,
    Ann Keehbauch, Joanie Schlafer
Prop Coordinator .... Denise J. Grillo
Prop Assistants .... Rebecca Haskins,
    Rashida Poole
Associate Costume Designer ....
.... Scott Traugott
Costume Design Assistants ....
.... Cory Ching, Rick Conway,
    Angela Kahler, Brian Russman
Associate Lighting Designer ....
.... Edward Pierce
Lighting Design Assistant ..... Karen Spahn
Assistant to Lighting Designer ....
.... Richard Swan
Automated Lighting Programmer ....
.... Aland Henderson
Automated Lighting Tracker ....
.... A. Cameron Zetty
Associate Sound Designer ..... John Shivers
Sound Design Assistants .... Jennifer Morris,
    Lisa Shriver
Hair Design Assistant .... Leslie Evers
Makeup Design Assistant ..... Richard Dean

Production Carpenter .... Jeff Goodman
Assistant Carpenter .... Mike Kearns
Fly Automation .... Dave Brown
Flyman .... Tim Welch
Deck Automation .... Ann Cavanaugh
Production Electrician ....
.... Salvatore J. Restuccia
Assistant Electrician .... David Trayer
Automated Lighting Technician ....
.... Brian Dawson
Lead Follow Spot Operator ...... Mike Lyons
Prop Supervisor .... Mike Smanko
Production Props .... Joe Redmond
Assistant Props .... Larry Clark
Production Sound Engineer ....
.... John Shivers
Sound Engineer .... Phil Lojo
Smoke and Atmospheric Effects ....
.... Chic Silber
Associate to Mr. Silber .... Bill McComb
Wardrobe Supervisor .... Terri Purcell
Assistant Wardrobe Supervisor ....
.... Nanette Golia

Dressers ... Ali Ahmidah, Charlie Catanese,
    Susan Checklick, Dana Davis, Melanie
    Hansen, Joby Horrigan, Joanne Kryszpin,
    Marcia McIntosh, David Mills,
    Duduzile Ndlovu, David Oliver,
    Jessica Scoblick, Jennifer Sorensen
Hair Supervisors .... Sonia Rivera
Hairdressers .... Gary Martori,
    Tod McKim, Lisa Thomas
Makeup Supervisor .... Jorge Vargas

Casting .... Bernard Telsey Casting,
    Bernie Telsey, Will Cantler, David Vaccari,
    Heidi Marshall, Lori Saposnick
Casting Associates ....
......Bethany Grace Berg, Victoria Pettibone
Casting Assistants .... Keisha Ames,
    Craig Burns
Developmental Casting Associates ....
.... Jack Bowdan, C.S.A.,
    Mark Brandon, Amy Kitts
Developmental Casting Assistant ....
.... Sarah Prosser

Music Preparation Supervisor ... Peter Miller,
    Miller Music Service
Assistant to Mr. Margoshes ....
.... Lawrence Rosen
Electronic Music Design & Programming .....
.... Music Arts Technologies, Inc.
Electronic Drum Programming ... Gary Seligson
Rehearsal Musicians .... Jim Abbott,
    Alf Bishai, Gary Seligson,
    Rob Mikulski, Dean Thomas

Merchandising ...... Buena Vista Theatrical
    Merchandise, L.L.C.,
    Christine Shelly, Linda Bessant,
    Mike Steinbrook, Kathleen Swift
Advertising .... Serino Coyne, Inc.
Press Associates ...... Adrian Bryan-Brown,
    Dennis Crowley, Erin Dunn,
    Amy Jacobs, Jamie Morris,
    Brian Rubin, Susanne Tighe
Press Assistants .... Rachel Applegate,
    Matt Kudish, Kila Packett,
    Matt Polk, Johnny Woodnal
Promotions .... The Marketing Group,
    Tanya Grubich, Laura Matalon, Ronni Seif
Production Photography .... Joan Marcus
Orthopedic Consultant ... Dr. Phillip Bauman
Production Travel .... Jackie Fooks,
    Carolyn Harms
Banking .... Barbara Von Borstel
Product Placement .... George Fenmore/
    More Merchandising International
Production Assistants ... Whitney Chapman,
    Clay Francis, Melanie Ganim,
    Adam Grosswirth, Ryan Mackey,
    David Reiersen
Production Interns .... Rachel Attridge,
    Erica Hemminger, John Hopkins,
    Catherine Lynch, Shannon Myers
Personal Assistant to Elton John ... Bob Halley
Assistant to Tim Rice .... Eileen Heinink
Special Thanks .... Lynn Beckemeyer,
    Harry Grossman

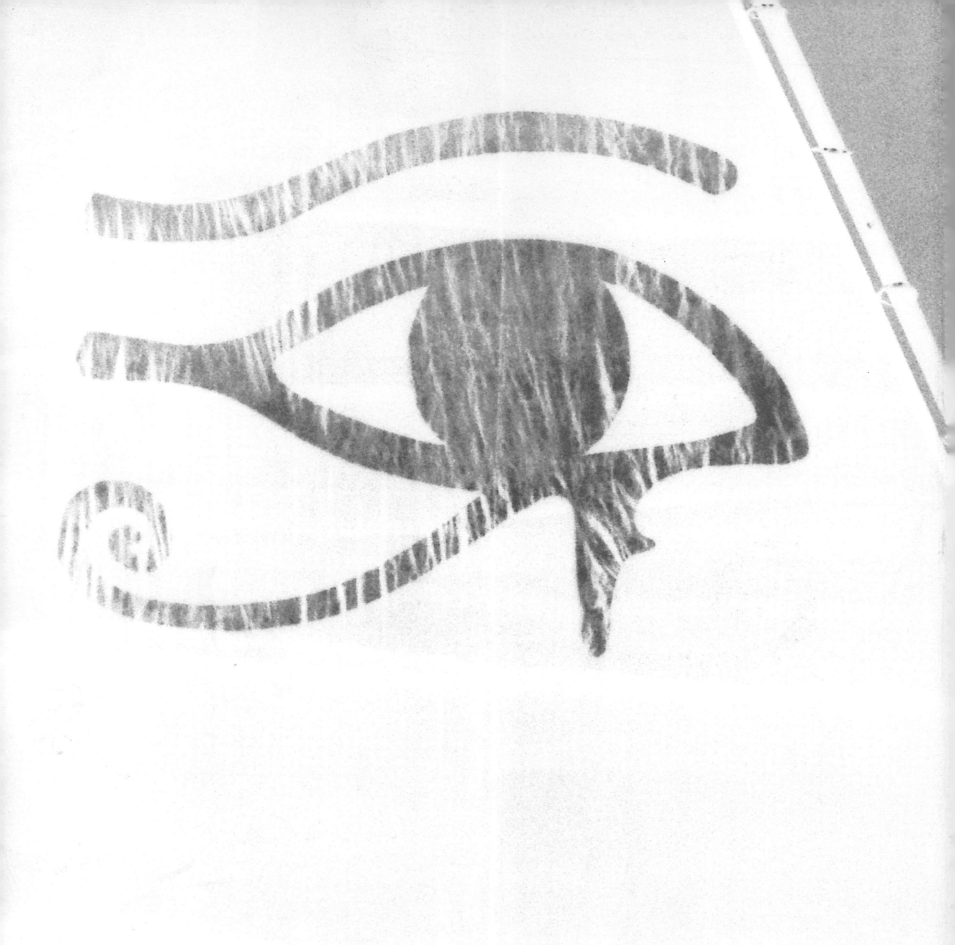